THE WAY OF THE EAGLE

BY

JERRY FANKHAUSER, M.S.W.

MIRACLE PUBLISHING COMPANY, INC.

ACKNOWLEDGEMENTS

I want to express my deep gratitude to the following people who have been such an important part of the unfolding of this book:

To **Dr. Kenneth Wapnick**, for his support and friendship, for being a mentor in understanding the principles of **A Course in Miracles**, and for the insights from his own personal writings.

To **Margo Skains**, publisher of this book, for her skill and talent in bringing it into print.

To **Pat Bonney**, for her loving support in editing and typing the manuscript.

To **Beverly Litton**, for her creative talent in drawing the cartoons in the book.

Miracle Publishing Company, Inc.
18 Charleston North
Sugarland, Texas 77478
713-242-4352

First printing, March, 1987

Manufactured in the United States of America

Cover design by Miracle Publishing

ISBN: 0-911197-10-9

OTHER BOOKS BY THE AUTHOR

FROM A CHICKEN TO AN EAGLE

THE POWER OF AFFIRMATIONS

EVERYBODY IS YOUR TEACHER

TABLE OF CONTENTS

THE WAY OF THE EAGLE

INTRODUCTION

The process of discovering who we really are can be very exciting. Writing one of my earlier books, **From a Chicken to an Eagle**, was part of my own process of unfolding and discovery. In a sense, I shared my own personal process with you, and, in the sharing, my own expansion took place. This new book is a continuation of this process. I hope that sharing my path in discovering my way home will be helpful and useful as you continue in your own personal unfoldment.

From a Chicken to an Eagle gave an overview of what I call the "chicken" and "eagle" philosophies and helped us see the real contrast between these two ways of looking at ourselves; in addition, it showed us the process we go through as we move out of the chicken yard.[1] The focus of the present book will be to describe the dynamics that undergird the structure of each philososphy. The first part of this book will give a step-by-step description of how the chicken philosophy was created and how it works; in the second part, we will learn how the eagle takes the very dynamics that keep us in the chicken yard and uses them to show us how to get out of the chicken yard and to come home to who we really are.

---

[1] If you have not read **From a Chicken to an Eagle**, you may find it helpful to do so, as it will supplement what you will be reading in this book.

THE CHICKEN AND THE EAGLE

One day a naturalist who was passing by a farm saw in the barnyard a flock of chickens, and among them was an eagle. The naturalist inquired of the owner why it was that an eagle, the king of all birds, should be reduced to living in the barnyard with the chickens.

"Since I have given it chicken feed and trained it to be a chicken, it has never learned to fly," replied the owner. "It behaves as chickens behave, so it no longer thinks of itself as an eagle."

"Still," insisted the naturalist, "it has the heart of an eagle and can surely be taught to fly."

After talking it over, the two men agreed to find out whether this was possible. Gently, the naturalist took the eagle in his arms and said, "You belong to the sky and not to the earth. Stretch forth your wings and fly."

The eagle, however, was confused; he did not know who he was. Seeing the chickens eating their food, he jumped down to be with them again.

Undismayed, the naturalist took the eagle on the following day up on the roof of the house and urged him again, saying, "You are an eagle. Stretch forth your wings and fly." But the eagle was afraid of his unknown self and the world and jumped down once more for the chicken food.

On the third day the naturalist rose early and took the eagle out of the barnyard to a high mountain. There he held the king of the birds high above him and encouraged him again, saying, "You are an eagle. You belong to the sky as well as the earth. Stretch forth your wings now and fly."

The eagle looked back towards the barnyard and up to the sky. Still he did not fly. Then the naturalist lifted him straight towards the sun, and it happened: the eagle began to tremble; slowly he stretched his wings. At last, with a triumphant cry he soared into the heavens.

It may be that the eagle still remembers the chickens with nostalgia; it may even be that he occasionally revisits the barnyard. But as far as anyone knows, he has never returned to lead the life of a chicken. He was an eagle, though he had been kept and tamed as a chicken.

And just like the eagle, people who have learned to think of themselves as something they aren't can re-decide in favor of what they really are.

The story of the eagle in the chicken yard is our story, a story about accepting something about ourselves that is not true — that we are chickens, unable to fly — and living as if it were true. We think we are chickens because we have accepted a perception about ourselves that is the chicken philosophy of life. In truth, we really are eagles with the potential to soar, to be free to experience our real essence: love, joy, peace, freedom. But alas, we find ourselves in the chicken yard feeling confused and fearful, and with no sense of life, purpose or direction.

Getting out of the chicken yard entails several steps. The first big step is to understand the dynamics of life in the chicken yard, where it came from, how it works and how it perpetuates itself. It is in the understanding of these dynamics that we see why we are stuck in a way of life that doesn't work.

The second step is to realize that we have assumed the chicken philosophy is the truth about ourselves and that we are living our lives on that assumption.

The third step is opening ourselves to the possibility that there is another way to live, a way that will no longer bring us fear, anger, guilt, confusion and suffering as the chicken philosophy does but will instead bring us the inner peace and love that make up the essence of who we are and were created to be.

The fourth step is to find that way by understanding how the eagle takes the insane system at work in the chicken yard and uses it to show us our path home. This path is called forgiveness.

The final step is to begin practicing forgiveness in our everyday lives, by moving the blocks of fear, anger and guilt out of the way so that who we really are, an Eagle, a child of Love, becomes obvious and clear.

PROLOGUE

Picture yourself sitting in your own internal movie theater. What you see on the screen is what you believe to be true about you as a person. If you are experiencing fear, anger, guilt or confusion, you are seeing yourself through the eyes or film of the chicken philosophy. This film has been running most of our lives, and we accept this as being the truth about ourselves. The theme of this film is that there is something basically wrong with me. I have a fatal flaw that is eternally fixed. What we see on this film is our effort to prove this is not true, but the ending of each story is the same: pain, suffering and separation, and a feeling of being lost and alone.

But there is another choice, another film available to us: the eagle film. The theme of this film is the Real Truth about ourselves, that we are Love, Peace, Joy, Freedom and Light. There is nothing to prove, only an acceptance of this Truth as being the Real Truth.

Because we have accepted and believe that what the chicken film tells us is true, we need a way of helping us to make the moment-to-moment choice to put on the eagle film. This way is called forgiveness, and by practicing this way of the eagle, we see the Real Truth not only about ourselves but about our brother.

This book describes how we have separated ourself from our Real Self, living alone and separ-ated in our own made up world, and how, through change and the practicing of forgiveness, we can go Home to that place of Peace, Love, and Joy.

PART I

THE WAY OF THE CHICKEN

Chicken Projection
CHICKEN FILM
THE TRUTH ABOUT YOU
A FEAR, ANGER, AND GUILT PRODUCTION
B. LITTON

CHAPTER 1

THE DYNAMICS OF THE CHICKEN PHILOSOPHY

Where did the chicken philosophy come from, what gave it birth, and how does it work? The birth and dynamics of the chicken philosophy can be found in the Bible story of Adam and Eve.

Picture with me Adam and Eve in the Garden of Eden. All their needs have been provided. God has told them that they can eat of the fruit of every tree except one, and they are to leave the fruit of this one alone. After talking it over, Adam and Eve decide through their own free will to eat of this forbidden tree.

However, the moment that Adam takes that first bite out of the apple, a strange thing happens in his mind. He realizes that he has done something he was told not to do, and, *in his own mind,* Adam decides that this thing he has done is wrong, that he has attacked God. In this way, the idea of sin is born. But remember, this is just an idea that he made up in his mind, just a thought. No one outside himself — and certainly not God — has accused him of anything.

Nevertheless, with this idea in his head that he has done something wrong, he now takes the next logical step and decides that there must be something basically wrong with him, that he is, in fact, a sinner. Two very important things have now happened: first, as we have seen, sin is born — entirely in Adam's mind, to be sure, but very real to him, nevertheless — and second, Adam feels suddenly separated from God. God is now Someone out there against whom Adam has committed this sin.

From this point, Adam's mind really begins to pick up speed. He has committed an unpardonable sin, and, naturally enough, feelings of guilt begin to stir within him. Thus, sin has sired guilt. And, of course, since Adam has started to feel guilty, it is only logical that his next thought is of punishment. Because he has disobeyed God, God must now be angry at him, and His punishment will be severe. (Again, keep in mind Adam is making all of this up in his mind.)

The thought of the punishment which must be in store for him now gives rise in Adam to a final emotion: Fear. Adam is afraid that God will take His vengeance out on him and it will be dreadful. Perhaps, worries Adam, God will strike him dead. Thus, in just a few simple and seemingly logical steps, we have watched Adam go from the peace and tranquility of his original state to a concept of himself as sinner, to feelings of guilt, worry over punishment, and finally fear of God.

Even though it has all been a fantasy that Adam is creating in his own mind, God is now seen as an avenger who seeks to punish His children for their crime. The God of Love has now been transformed into a God of fear, and the peace that is our natural inheritance has become terror, anxiety, and a defensiveness that keeps us on guard against a

Father that we believe we have attacked and who will therefore attack us.

This brings us back to that idea of separation from God that has gotten a firm foothold in Adam's madly racing thoughts. Once Adam begins to perceive this Father through guilt and fear, inevitably he begins to feel that, if he lets the Father back into his life, he will be struck dead by His fury as punishment for his attack on Him. And so, of course, Adam starts to feel a strong need to hide from God.

Now, logically, we can only hide from someone or something else if we are separate from that other person or thing. So clearly, we see that Adam has created a sense of himself as apart from God; he has in effect created a false self (the chicken), and from this new perception of himself as separate, he hears a voice (the chicken's voice) telling him that, because he is guilty of this terrible act, he has become a terrible creature.

Kenneth Wapnick, a psychologist who has written extensively about this process, has summed it up in this way: "The feeling of unworthiness, inadequacy, and inferiority from which we suffer stems from the underlying sense of guilt, of some wrongdoing that can never be corrected; some basic 'wrongness' in ourselves that can never be healed."[2] Now we think of ourselves as sinners, just as Adam did. This is our essence. It is this belief that we are inherently and unforgivably sinful, that there is

---

[2] Kenneth Wapnick

something basically wrong with us, which constitutes the basic dynamics of the chicken philosophy. We are sinners, therefore we should feel guilty. Because we are sinners, we will be punished. Because we will be punished, we are afraid.

It is time, now, to take a closer look at each of these aspects of the chicken philosophy, sin, guilt, punishment, and fear, to find out how each one works in our lives.

* * *

Sin

Remember, throughout our whole discussion of Adam's experience in the Garden, we were careful to point out that the sin he felt he had committed existed only in his mind. God never placed that label on Adam's act of eating the apple — Adam did, and because he did, he had to accept the consequence of the label, which was to see himself as separate from God. The idea of sin, then, and the separation which followed from it, existed only as thoughts that Adam held in his mind.

In exactly the same way, sin for us is just the *thought* of separation. It is a *thought* that we have accepted as the truth about ourselves. It is a *belief* that we can create a self separate from the Creator. It is an *idea* that denies who we really are. We can never not be who we are, children of Love, but we can deny that we are children of Love and create the illusion of another self.

Remember, Adam just made up in his mind that he had done something wrong and that he had sinned and now was a sinner. Sin is only the *thought* of separation.

* * *

Guilt

If Adam sinned then it must follow that he will feel guilty because he has done something wrong, he has attacked God. This guilt, this feeling that something is inherently wrong with him at the core of his very being, is so deep that Adam feels he will never be forgiven and is beyond the love of God.

Similarly, having condemned ourselves as sinners for whatever the act, we become laden with guilt. We feel that we are such poor excuses for human beings that not only could no other person ever respect us or love us, but certainly God will want nothing more to do with us. Again, Kenneth Wapnick has described the situation as we imagine it:

> *Guilt may be associated with the experience of ourselves as physical and psychological beings in various ways, self-hatred, self-doubt, a gnawing awareness of inferiority and insecurity, feelings of incompletion, unfulfillment, lack, and a belief in one's personal failure before oneself, others and God.*
>
> *Each of us is more than familiar with feeling guilty over things in our past. The history of our individual lives can be seen, from this point of view, to be a litany to our guilt over what we have done or not done, said or not said, thought or not thought. We feel guilty because we picked on a younger sibling, were caught stealing candy from the neighborhood store, cut school to go fishing or*

watch a baseball game, or were punished by the teacher for talking in class or not doing homework. As adults we feel guilty for being unkind to someone in need, having lost our temper, cheating on our income tax, not being faithful to the commandments, failing to perform prescribed religious rituals, or for harboring sexual feelings toward people forbidden by standards of morality.[3]

The list is endless. If we could see all of those things we have done and left undone about which we feel guilty, it would just be the tip of the iceberg. These instances of guilt only reflect a much deeper experience of unworthiness and inadequacy and sense of lack. Just as the greater part of an iceberg rests beneath the surface of the water, so does the bulk of our guilt rest in our unconscious minds, out of our conscious awareness. These feelings of guilt are so deep that we believe there is no way we can be free of them.

Let me give you an example of how unconscious our guilt is. Remember the last time you were driving your automobile past a radar trap manned by a policeman. You were not speeding, you were doing nothing wrong, but you felt guilty. Or remember the last time someone gave you a compliment, and you felt embarrassed, guilty. You were feeling unworthy of the compliment because at some level you felt that it was not true about you and that, if people only knew the truth, they wouldn't be complimenting you.

---

[3] Kenneth Wapnick, **Forgiveness and Jesus**, Foundation for A Course in Miracles, Crompond, N.Y., 1983, p. 18.

Guilt is the way the chicken perpetuates its system. In the chicken philosophy, we base our lives on the belief that there is a lack in us, that something is basically wrong with us. We have done something so bad, we have sinned so horribly, that God will eternally be mad at us. As we will see later, in the chicken system we spend our lives trying not to be bad or wrong, and trying to find ways to get back in good with God.

* * *

Punishment and Fear

Once Adam had become convinced of his guilt, we have seen how naturally it followed that he would begin to dread punishment and the terrible things that he determined God must have in store for him. And, as he considered the form this punishment might take, fear was born. We believe, as Adam did, that we have attacked God by opposing Him; therefore, we believe, He is justified in attacking us in return.

We now picture God as a wrathful, avenging Father, who will punish us by striking us dead or something equally severe. In fact, we can turn back to the Bible and see this very thing seeming to happen to Adam and Eve, when God places His well-known curses on them:

> *Because you have done this . . . I will multiply your pains in childbearing; you shall give birth to your children in pain. . . . Because you . . .*

> *ate from the tree of which I had forbidden you to eat, accursed be the soil because of you. With suffering shall you get your food from it every day of your life. . . . With sweat on your brow shall you eat your bread, until you return to the soil as you were taken from it. For dust you are and to dust you shall return.*[4]

Pain, suffering and death are now the punishment for doing this awful deed of disobeying God. It is no wonder that our fear of this avenging, wrathful Father and His awful curses becomes so terrifying that we are no longer able to deal with it in our conscious minds. Instead, we must push it down into the unconscious level, which carries on a nightmarish life, seemingly independent of our conscious experience. We do not realize that our fear, which seems to come into our minds from the world outside of us, really begins with the unconscious belief in sin, which creates guilt, which demands punishment, which, unconsciously, we believe we deserve.

Moreover, this underlying fear of punishment is felt with any authority figure, whether it be a parent, teacher, boss or even God himself. We can even feel we are being punished by institutions such as the government (particularly the Internal Revenue Service!) or religious organizations, or even by natural occurrences, such as the weather.

Thus, once we have accepted guilt into our minds, we cannot avoid fear. The belief in our guilt at having done something wrong toward God leads

---

[4] Genesis 3:14, 16, 17, 19.

us to expect reprisal, so we live our lives in constant fear that some sort of tragedy or catastrophe is just around the next corner. This process has great psychological validity for us, as Wapnick once again shows:

> *We may understand this dynamic of sin, guilt and fear as a unity. The belief in our inherent wrongness or sinfulness leads to our experience of guilt over who we are; and this leads us to fear the punishment we believe we deserve and will receive. This unholy trinity is truly a psychological hell and constitutes the ego (chicken self). It is the separated self with which we identify, and consequently on which we base our beliefs, judgments, and perceptions. The world that arises from this self is a world of terror from which there seems to be no escape.*[5]

Let me summarize the condition of separation in a different form. The moment that Adam (who represents all mankind) chose to eat of the apple, the idea of separation was established in his mind in the form of a dream of separation. This dream was one where Adam was sinful and wrong, where guilt, punishment and fear were basic principles, where God was turned into an angry, wrathful Father, and where the result of the dream was pain, suffering and death. This is your dream and my dream. We believe this dream is the truth about us and God, and as all of us know, dreams can feel very real.

It is interesting to note that the Bible says a deep sleep fell upon Adam, and nowehere is there a

[5] Wapnick, **Forgiveness and Jesus**, p. 26.

reference to his waking up. We are all dreaming the same dream of separation as Adam did and living our lives on the principles of this dream. But the possibility of awakening is always open to us. As the Course in Miracles says, "You are at home in God, dreaming of exile but perfectly capable of awakening to reality."[6]

---

[6] Text, **A Course in Miracles**, Foundation for Inner Peace, Tiburon, California, p. 169.

CHAPTER 2

THE CHICKEN'S WAY OUT (DENIAL AND PROJECTION)

Back to our story. When we left Adam, he had made up in his mind that he had done something wrong, that he was a sinner; he now felt guilty and was afraid God would strike him dead when He found out. With all of this weighing him down, he can see only one course of action open to him, and he takes it: he immediately goes and hides in the bushes. Adam believes he is the new self (the chicken) he has made up, and so, naturally, he acts as if this is now the truth about who he is.

Because of this overwhelming guilt and fear, Adam now needs someone to turn to for help. He needs protection against this fear that he will be struck dead. He cannot turn to God because he has made Him the enemy who is going to judge and punish him. The only one left to turn to is the chicken.

The first suggestion the chicken makes to Adam is that he must not get too close to his guilt, because the closer he comes to it the more fearful it will make him and the closer he will be to the wrath of God. What the chicken doesn't tell Adam is that the fear he is trying to get away from is really the chicken's fear. The chicken is afraid that, if Adam were to get close to God again, he would see God as He truly is, a loving Father who has no intention of punishing Adam or even of condemning him. Once

Adam discovered that, he would no longer be afraid, he would let go of the chicken, and the chicken would disappear. So the chicken has a very strong investment in feeding and nourishing Adam's fear — upon it depends the chicken's very existence.

So Adam, stuck in his dream of separation from God, looks on the chicken as his only hope. To help Adam out of his overwhelming experience of guilt, the next step which the chicken employs consists, actually, of two basic dynamics; denial (also called repression) and projection. These two elements are the bulwark of the chicken system and are what holds this way of thinking together.

The chicken begins this part of his treatment by suggesting that Adam handle his guilt by denying or repressing it. "Push it out of your awareness, pretend it is not really there, push it into the unconscious," is the cry of the chicken. It is like the ostrich who sticks his head in the sand and has the magical hope that if he doesn't see whatever upsets him, it does not exist. Who of us has not, while cleaning our house, swept some dirt under the rug hoping that, because it's out of sight, it is out of mind and we can have the illusion of a clean house.

Denial is a very powerful process. As a psychotherapist, I see it in action everyday in my office. A wife sits with her husband and tells me how unhappy she is in the relationship. Her husband declares that he is very happy in the relationship and does not see that there is a problem. A business man complains to me that his business is close to bankruptcy, yet he firmly denies that what he is doing isn't working. A mother whose son has been arrested several times has convinced herself — and tries to convince me — that her son does not have a problem.

This is, in fact, exactly how denial can be such a powerful tool for us: it makes us able to overlook the obvious — sometimes for a long period of time. And if we can't see a problem — or refuse to see it — we certainly don't have to deal with it. And so we think we're off the hook. But denial only works up to a point. We still have a haunting inner awareness that the problem is still there. The carpet under which we are sweeping our dirt is getting lumpy, and sooner or later, we find ourselves tripping over one or another of the lumps, as a reminder that we are hiding something.

But just as soon as we begin to feel this discomfort, there is our old friend, the chicken, coming to our rescue again with what is the ultimate solution. First we deny our guilt; then we project it. Projection is the chicken's most effective weapon in his efforts to keep us from seeing that there is really nothing to be afraid of — but, of course, he doesn't tell us this. Instead, he insinuates that we can rid ourselves of our guilt if we simply take our problems and put the responsibility for them on someone or something else. We literally hurl our problems away from us and project them "out there" away from ourselves.

In this way, we have not only removed our problems from our awareness, but we now are convinced our problems are really not ours but have instead come from outside ourselves. Now, says the chicken, our problems are solved. We no longer have to experience that guilt as our own, because we have projected it onto agents outside ourselves. "They" are now the guilty parties, the source of our unhappiness. "They" are responsible for the unpleasant things that have happened to us, and of course, "they" need to be punished.

Let's go back to our story to see how this works for Adam. When God discovers Adam and Eve hiding, He asks them the simple question, "Who ate the apple?" Sure enough, Adam, feeling guilty as we have seen, now denies the responsibility for his actions and projects his guilt on Eve. "Eve made me do it; it's really her fault." Of course Eve, being just as human as Adam, continues the process by denying her participation and projecting the blame and guilt onto the snake. "The snake made me do it," she is quick to point out. Thus, by putting the blame on someone or something else, Adam and Eve have the illusion that the guilt has been handled and is no longer a threat. They are off the hook.

Indeed, this technique seems to work so well for Adam and Eve that it becomes the normal way to deal with guilt and fear. By the time we come to the 16th chapter of the book of Leviticus, projection has almost become institutionalized, and Kenneth Wapnick gives us a beautiful explanation of the ritual that it has evolved into:

> *On the Day of Atonement (Yom Kippur), the purification of the children of Israel was to be accomplished through two ritual acts: the intercession of the high priest who performed certain ritualistic sacrifices in the sanctuary, followed by the selection of a goat, on*

> *which "Aaron [the priest] must lay his hands on its head and confess all the faults of the sons of Israel. . . . and lay them to its charge. Having thus laid them on the goat's head, he shall send it out into the desert . . . and the goat will bear all their faults away with it and into a desert place" (Lev. 16:21f). The sins of the people have thus been transferred to (projected onto) the goat who is driven away, symbolically acting out the ego [chicken's] maladaptive method of absolving us from our sins.*[7]

This is where the term "scapegoat" comes from, and although we today may not use this literal ceremony nor even be familiar with it, we are quite familiar with the technique itself.

Once Adam and Eve had projected the responsibility for their "sin" onto the snake, the snake naturally became the "bad guy." And, as we know, down through history, snakes have pretty consistently gotten a bad press. In the same way, once we have projected our guilt and blame on someone else, we want to put as much distance between ourselves and those sins as we can. We must demonstrate to ourselves and others that we are not guilty, that someone else is the "guilty one." We do this by becoming angry at that "guilty party." This anger very effectively distances us from the person or agent we have projected upon and also becomes our attempt to justify the projection of our guilt.

As we proceed down this path which takes us farther and farther from the truth, we see that the chicken will stop at nothing to help us reinforce our choice of the guilty party. We create evidence, real or

---

[7] Kenneth Wapnick, **Forgiveness and Jesus**, p. 32.

imagined,to substantiate our projection. "Look at the terrible things you have done to me," we say. "Because of them I am unhappy and suffering." As often as we can, we repeat, "Look at your sins and feel guilty." What is not being said but what, in truth, underlies that anger is this: "Look at your sins and feel guilty because in this way I have freed myself of my sins and guilt." We can relax now, under the illusion that we have handled our guilt.

But alas we have been fooled. While the chicken tells us that anger and attack will rid us of our guilt we do not realize that projection, while it seems to give us a way out of our guilt, in reality reinforces it. Whenever we put guilt on someone else, no matter how we express it, the act will always involve attack, and if we attack, we will always feel guilty.

Now we have a vicious cycle. We feel guilty and attacked, and so we transfer our guilt onto someone else through projection, thinking we have rid ourselves of it. But what happens inside is that we feel more guilt because of our attack, so our original guilt is increased by our projection. The guiltier we feel, the more we need to deny and attack; the more we attack, the guiltier we feel, and so on and on and on. The basic overall cycle is self-perpetuating and becomes an unending process, one which reinforces itself and gains more and more power as it proceeds. We can see this graphically in Figure 1 on the next page.

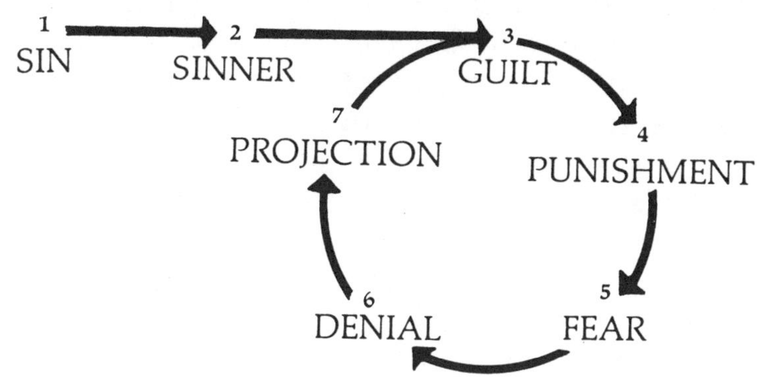

Figure 1

Yet even though we accept the chicken's method of handling our guilt, we know deep inside that we are attacking falsely and that the true problem is not in the other person but only in ourselves. The chicken, in order to continue its existence, must direct us to maintain a feeling of separation from our brothers and sisters so that we see them as different. The world now becomes a place where separation is the basis for existence.

However, while we live in this world of separation and are affected by it, we are responsible for our own reactions to the world and to anything that happens to us. Our inner experience is created by us. This is a very powerful concept, and understanding it is the first step in ending this self-perpetuating cycle. We will examine it in depth in the next chapter.

For now, though, as we conclude our examination of how the chicken's system originated and operates, we need to be aware of several factors. First, the chicken system is a very logical system and if we accept its basic premise, that we are sinners and guilty, then the rest will follow in a logical sequence. The chicken system does make sense and has an understandable structure. The only problem is, it doesn't work.

Second, let us never underestimate the chicken's purpose in trying to perpetuate its way of life. Its purpose is to reinforce guilt, suffering, and fear, and its ultimate gift to us is death. The chicken's behavior operates between suspiciousness and viciousness, and the closer we come to being willing to look at our guilt and the more we desire to see what is behind it, which is God's love, the more vicious the chicken will become. The desire it has to keep us fearful of our death, which it wants us to see as inevitable, comes from the fear of its own death, which is inevitable once we really see the Truth. If we wake up, the dream (and with it, the chicken) will disappear.

CHAPTER 3

HOW THE CHICKEN PHILOSOPHY IS ESTABLISHED IN OUR MINDS

Let's take another look at this process we've been discussing, this time in the step-by-step manner laid out in Diagram 1 on the following page. It begins when we first imagine ourselves to be sinners and is reinforced at every turn by the chicken's insidious promptings and suggestions, which lead us into fear and from there to denial and projection.

As we look at these steps, each one leading us inevitably to the next one, until we are caught up in a truly vicious cycle, we can only wonder how we could allow such a disheartening and discouraging process to become established in our personal world. It seems we ought to be able to see what is happening to us and stop it, nip it in the bud. Why is it that we let the chicken's philosophy become the program for our life?

To answer this question, we must first answer an even more basic one: How do we make decisions about anything? Obviously, we make our decisions and choices based upon our assessment of the information we receive. But — and here is the basic question we are really asking — how does information get inside of us? In other words, how does what's happening outside become internalized? The answer: through the five senses — seeing, hearing, tasting, smelling and touching. Let us examine how it all begins.

SIN ⇩	The thought of separation from God.
SINNER ⇩	We feel that something is inherently wrong with us: we have a fatal flaw.
GUILT ⇩	Based on our sense of inherent unworthiness; the feeling that is experienced in relation to sin.
PUNISHMENT ⇩	We feel we need to be punished because of our sin of separation against God.
FEAR ⇩	Originates in the expected punishment for our sins and the terror we feel about what God will do to us.
DENIAL ⇩	Avoiding our guilt by sweeping it under the rug, pretending the problem does not exist.
PROJECTION ⇩	Ridding ourselves of guilt by putting responsibility for our sins on someone or something else. The cause of our problems is now outside of ourselves.
GUILT ⇩	And the cycle continues. . . .

Diagram 1

When we were babies, it appears we were like little metal balls. Every stimulation from the outer world, whether a sight, a sound, a taste, a smell, or a touch, when it reached us, was like a tap on that metal ball. Whenever something tapped on that metal ball, a little "dit," a little impulse, would go up our nerves until it reached our brain.

In a recent article in **Science 81**, this process is explained using a slightly different analogy: "The senses are the brain's scouts; they bring in bits of the outside world. Each sense has its own range and specific sensitivity to external stimuli. The eye responds to light, the ear to sound, touch to texture and pressure. How the brain interprets the information the senses deliver to it is perception." [8]

The important thing to realize about this process of perception, then, is that, from the start, all the information that our brain receives is just a series of dit-dit-dits. The first task for the brain is to make up an interpretation of what these dits mean. Let us remember the brain is blind. It does not see what the eye sees; it merely receives the impulses the eye sends to it and makes up an interpretation or belief about the world "out there," which is based on those dits. Basically this is how we learn to see, and the process is the same for the other four senses.

In the article from **Science 81** just referred to, the author tells of a man who had been blind from birth but who, nevertheless, had acquired the skill of

---

[8] Nancy Hechinger, "Seeing Without Eyes," **Science 81**, March, 1981, p. 40.

using a lathe. At the age of fifty-three, this man had an operation which made it possible for him to see for the first time in his life. He soon recovered from the operation and was able to return to operating his lathe. But when he was taken into the room where the lathe was located and was now able to see the machine with his eyes, he didn't know what it was. He was not able to recognize it by sight, even though he was very familiar with it by touch. Of course, when he closed his eyes and touched the lathe, he recognized it immediately. But he needed to learn to coordinate the new information he was now receiving from his eyes with the interpretations that already existed in his brain based on what his sense of touch had been telling him about the world. He had to be taught how to see.

It is not hard to see why we soon begin to think that reality is outside of us. In truth, however, reality for each of us becomes what we have made up in our heads based on the dits we have received from the outside world. These dits provide information which we turn into beliefs and interpretations about who we think we are. Thus, each of us is really a bundle of beliefs talking to other bundles of beliefs, each feeling our own beliefs are really true.

Our made-up assumptions have now become the basis of who we think we really are, and from these we each begin to create our own history as individuals, which reinforce the basic assumptions we have made up about ourselves. Figure 2 on the next page describes this process:

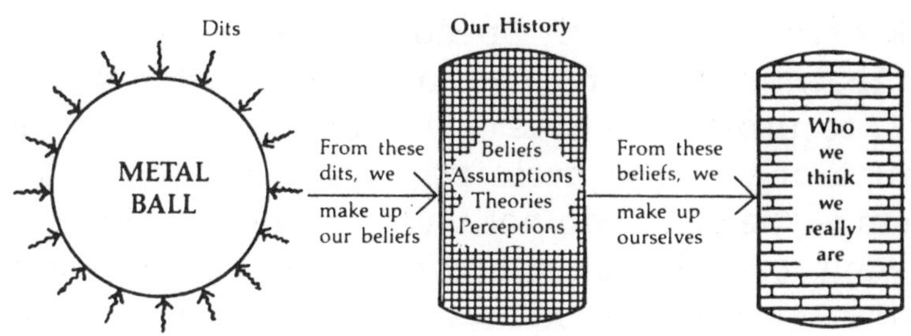

Figure 2

As the history of ourselves grows (as more and more dits reach our brains and are added to the beliefs and interpretations already there), we then see that we must begin to agree with those around us that certain series of dits mean certain things or else we set up the possibility of rejection. As a result, we continually re-create our world and re-arrange its beliefs so that they match up with those found in the chicken philosophy.

What we think we are now comes from a bundle of beliefs or assumptions that is our history, and we live our lives out of those beliefs as if they were the Truth about ourselves. We now have become the creators of who we think we are. We have kicked God off His throne, and now we have decided who we are. Of course, the new king we place on the throne to be in charge of ourselves is the chicken.

Our lives now become nothing more than the repetition of this guilt-ridden, fearful history over and over, and because we believe this is the real truth, we keep trying to find ways to make this set of beliefs work. We will possibly spend our entire lives trying this, that, or the other method to make this system work, to prove it is true. The joke is really on us, because one of the basic principles of the chicken system is "Seek and do not find."[9] The chicken does not want us to find anything; he just wants us to keep looking. Moreover, he wants us to keep looking outside of ourselves for our happiness, because he knows it's not there and, in this way, the chicken can keep his system going. Most people will have to try all alternatives — some of them a number of times — and come up empty before they see that the chicken system doesn't work. In effect, they have to bankrupt their system. The following is an example of this process.

The way we believe our lives will be happy. . . (the chicken philosophy).

10 — The results of following this path.

Figure 3

[9] See Jerry Fankhauser, **From a Chicken to an Eagle**, p. 8, for elaboration.

The circle in Figure 3 represents the chicken philosophy, that which we have accepted as true about life, relationships, and ourselves. The numbers in the circle represent the path by which we are to travel if we want to get what the chicken promises. These numbers add up to ten, which represents the promised results, the happiness and joy the chicken says will be ours if we follow his advice.

With high hopes, we follow the steps recommended by the chicken instructions in our daily lives, denying and projecting, blaming those people and things around us for whatever problems we encounter, and expecting that, any day now, happiness will be ours. But what we find instead, the results represented by the number 10, is that this way of looking at life doesn't work and only brings us pain and suffering and disappointment.

However, instead of realizing that the system doesn't work, we think that there is something wrong with us, that we aren't doing it right, that we aren't trying hard enough. And the chicken is right there with advice: "Let's just try another '-ism' or '-osophy' [that puts a different pattern into the background of our lives, represented by pattern within the circle], and let's rearrange the order of the steps we should follow [that mixes the same old numbers up so that now they are in a different order]. This'll do the trick — happiness is right around the corner." So we try once again, seemingly doing something different, and we keep looking for that elusive pot of gold, the peace and happiness the chicken assures us is just ahead. Our "new" system now looks like Figure 4:

Picture looks different, but the result is the same.

10 — still results in pain and suffering.

Figure 4

Now we say to ourselves, "If I had only done this — or just hadn't done that — it would have worked." So we try yet another way. We use the same system, the same numbers, but we arrange them in yet another sequence and put yet another pattern into the background. And, predictably, the result is still the same, seeking but never finding:

Another try —

Result? Still 10. . .

Figure 5

This process of seeking and never finding will go on until we reach the point where, no matter what combination of numbers and backgrounds we try, we realize that it just isn't working for us. At that point, we have bankrupted the system. No matter how we try, we can no longer see any way that this system of thinking will work.

A typical example of this process can be seen in people who go through relationship after relationship, trying to make each of them work but always achieving the same results: pain, suffering, and disappointment. Such people feel that, if they just try hard enough, whatever they are doing will eventually be successful, and they will finally be part of a successful relationship. But such a belief has as much chance of success as trying over and over again to arrange two and two in such a way that they will add up to five.

As a psychotherapist, I have found that it's not unusual for a couple to be sitting in my office describing to me the mess they have created. Then both will stop and look at me and ask, "What do you think is wrong?" I simply say to them, "What both of you are doing doesn't work." Their reply is almost always the same, "That's too simple." What they want me to do is to show them what it is that they are doing within their system that is wrong. They think that if they can just find out where they missed the boat, then they can go back, correct that step, and this time through, everything will come out right. They are essentially trying to figure out craziness, and if you try to figure out craziness, you have bought into craziness and you just become more crazy.

By "craziness" here, I am referring to actions someone continues to perform over and over again, though those actions are not working, and the only results from those actions are pain and suffering. Now, at this point, there is good news and bad news. The bad news is that, if we continue to live our lives in this way, based on this history which we think is true but which is not, we will just receive more of the same old history. We will just continue seeking but not finding.

There is a poem, "The Calf-Path," by Sam Walter Foss, which, in an insightful and amusing way, really sums up what I have been saying:

THE CALF-PATH

One day, through the primeval wood,
A calf walked home, as good calves should:
But made a trail all bent askew,
A crooked trail, as all calves do.

The trail was taken up next day
By a lone dog that passed that way;
And then a wise bellwether sheep
Pursued the trail o'er vale and steep,
And drew the flock behind him, too,
As good bellwethers do.

And from that day, o'er hill and glade,
Through those old woods a path was made;
And many folks wound in and out,
And dodged, and turned, and bent about
And uttered words of righteous wrath
Because 'twas such a crooked path.

But still they followed — do not laugh —
The first migrations of that calf.

This crooked lane became a road,
Where many a poor horse with his load
Toiled on beneath the burning sun,
And traveled some three miles in one.
And thus a century and a half
They trod the footsteps of that calf.

The road, before they were aware,
Became a crowded thoroughfare;
And soon the central street was this
Of a renowned metropolis;
And people two centuries and a half
Trod in the footsteps of that calf.

They followed still his crooked way,
And lost one hundred years a day;
For thus such reverence is lent
To well-established precedent.

A moral lesson this might teach,
Were I ordained and called to preach;
For people are prone to go it blind
Along the calf-paths of the mind,
And work away from sun to sun
To do what others have always done.

They follow in the beaten track,
And out and in, and forth and back,
And still their devious course pursue,
To keep the path that others do.

But how the wise old wood-gods laugh,
Who saw the first primeval calf!

— Sam Walter Foss (1858-1911)

Bankrupting the chicken system is a basic prerequisite for moving toward choosing the eagle to be a guide for our lives. I am reminded of a session I had with a fifty-year-old woman with whom I had been working. She had come to the realization that nothing was working for her. Greatly discouraged, she said to me, "I have made a mess of my life. Nothing works, and I guess I'm a total failure."

"No, you aren't a failure at all. You are really a success," I said. She looked at me, very puzzled, as I went on. "You are not a failure; you are a success. You are successful at doing something that doesn't work, and until you are successful at that, you will never want to look at another way of doing it."

An illustration provided by Professor Martin Hellman of Stanford University sums up the results of following the chicken philosophy. Prof. Hellman is a mathematician internationally recognized for his expertise in statistics, probability and cryptography. He describes the use of a mathematical process called the "two-step Markov principle" and explains it in terms of Russian roulette:

> *In Russian roulette, you take a revolver with six chambers and load only one. You spin the cylinder, place the barrel against your brain, and pull the trigger. There is one chance in six of getting killed. But that's if you play the game only one time. If you play twice, the two chances of being shot reinforce each other, and the odds are almost one in three of killing yourself. After 10 trials the odds are 84% that you're dead; after 20 trials, 97%. And if you continue to play, the odds become 100% that you will shoot yourself. It's inevitable. In*

> *mathematics, we say it happens "with probability one." It's certain.*
>
> *It doesn't matter if your gun has six chambers or 60 or 600. The smaller probability of killing yourself at each trial prolongs the game, but it does not change the outcome. You still get shot with probability one.*[10]

In truth, we can keep trying to play the chicken's game, following his philosophy, which we will do because that's all we've learned. But the outcome will always be the same: it won't work. It will only bring us pain and suffering.

And that leads us to the good news. If we are just a series of interpretations and beliefs, then there must be a self that makes the decision to see life in whatever way it is that each of us has decided is real. That same self can choose to see from a different perspective. The power in our lives is activated the moment we begin to *choose*, instead of just following the dictates of our history. To choose is to move into the realm of possibility, where we can base our choices on whether the results work. We now have the opportunity to choose who will be on the throne of our lives. The possibility of choosing the eagle is now present.

The power in our lives comes when we begin to choose, not just to follow the program. The joy in our lives comes when we begin choosing the Eagle as the guide to our lives.

---

[10] "Nuclear War Is Inevitable — Unless. . . ," **Parade Magazine,** August 24, 1986, p. 17.

Eagle Production
EAGLE FILM
A HEALING PRODUCTION
THE TRUTH ABOUT YOU!
STARRING
LOVE AND FORGIVENESS
B. LITTON

PART II

THE WAY OF THE EAGLE

CHAPTER 4

THE DYNAMICS OF THE EAGLE'S PHILOSOPHY

Just as the chicken had a Bible story that described its perception, so does the eagle. The eagle's story, which begins where the story of Adam and Eve leaves off, is the parable of the Prodigal Son (Luke 15:11-24). Adam, remember, first got the idea in his head that he was separate from his Creator. The prodigal son, too, thought the thought of separation but carried it even further, thinking that he could go off by himself and create his own kingdom, create a new self independent of his Father.

Of course, he went through all of the stages that we are learning to expect — sin, guilt, fear of punishment, denial and projection — only to find that the world he had created was one of pain and suffering, one in which he himself wound up living with the pigs. He tried all of the alternatives in trying to make his world work and came to the point of bankruptcy. He came to a point described by one of my patients who had bankrupted her own chicken system: "I'm sick and tired of being sick and tired."

Finally, realizing his hopeless situation and having literally nowhere else to go, the prodigal son decides to go Home. The Bible says, "He came to himself."

But he has a problem: the chicken, the "God" he has created for himself and believes in desperately, is telling him that, if he goes home, wrath and vengeance will be meted out to him. Yet, at the same time, there is something inside of the prodigal son, another voice, much quieter but just as insistent, that keeps telling him this is not true. This voice reminds him that the Father is really a loving Father and will welcome him home.

Thus, as he starts home, his confusion is evident: on the one hand, there is the loud voice of the chicken, telling him how angry his Father will be, that going home is a mistake because he will be struck dead with the vengeance of an angry Father. But on the other hand, if he listens intently, he can hear that still, small voice telling him of a loving Father, one who will understand and not condemn.

"What can I do so my Father won't be so mad," wonders the prodigal son, in his confusion. Then an idea comes to him: "I will give up my birthright as a son and ask my Father if I can just be a servant in His house. Maybe if I punish myself this way, then He won't be so hard on me." As he draws closer and closer to home, he can almost be heard practicing out loud what he will say so as not to offend his Father.

And then, when he can just begin to make out his Father's house far off in the distance, and when the voice of the chicken, with its warnings of danger and doom, has reached a panic level, he looks ahead into that distance, and he can suddenly see someone, arms outstretched, running toward him. Incredibly, it is his Father. Imagine the shock he must feel at this moment, expecting an angry reception and instead arriving home to have his Father welcome him with joy and celebration.

The still, small voice was right from the start. And, in the light of the loving Father, the chicken's perception of anger and vengeance vanishes, because that perception was never true; it was merely an idea created and existing only in the mind of the prodigal son. When he brought his darkness of sin, guilt, and fear into the light of the Father, the darkness was nowhere to be seen.

At this point, we can clearly and concisely summarize the difference between the dynamics of the chicken and the dynamics of the eagle. The chicken tells us that we have sinned and are sinners, that we should feel guilty for our actions, that God is no longer our protector but rather will punish us for having attacked Him. The eagle, however, tells us that we have not sinned nor separated ourselves from God, but that we have simply made a mistake in perception. Moreover, there is no punishment involved because of this mistake; all that is needed is for us to correct the perception. The following illustrates this point.

CHICKEN	EAGLE
SIN	MISTAKE IN PERCEPTION
⇩	⇩
PUNISHMENT	CORRECTION IN PERCEPTION

Diagram 2

Let us remember that these two systems are diametrically opposed to each other. Part of the confusion we have had throughout history has come from the attempt to merge these systems into one. We first read about the God of the Old Testament, a God of anger and vengeance, and then we turn a few pages and find that same God in the New Testament, only now He is a loving Father. It is impossible to reconcile these two images. Just as you can't have a little bit of hell in heaven or a little bit of heaven in hell, you cannot merge an angry father who is going to punish you with a loving Father who totally accepts you just as He created you. One image must be true, one must be false. And, in fact, one system, the eagle's, is true, Truth with a capital "T," and one system, the chicken's, is false, an illusion.

Let me illustrate this contrast. When we accept the program of the chicken, it is as if we are sitting inside of a fort that we have created for our own protection. Our fort is being attacked by Indians, and we are waiting for the cavalry to come and save us. I have some good news and some bad news. The bad news is that the cavalry is not coming. The good news is that there aren't any Indians.

Fear, anger, and guilt are the "Indians" that we have imagined are attacking our fort, and as we bring the darkness of fear, anger, and guilt into the light of the eagle, they disappear. The eagle tells us that we need not live in our fort, hiding from an angry father. The Truth is that there is a loving Father waiting for us to come home, waiting to throw His arms around us and celebrate our return from the far country.

Forgiveness
Production
EAGLE FILM
THE TRUTH
ABOUT YOUR
BROTHER!
STARRING
LOVE AND FORGIVENESS
A HEALING PRODUCTION
BEVERLY LITTON

CHAPTER 5

FORGIVENESS: THE WAY HOME (AN OVERVIEW)

The unexpected element in the prodigal son's homecoming is forgiveness. Expecting punishment, he finds only freely flowing love. Feeling almost overwhelmed by guilt, he is met with not a word of reproach, of anger, of judgment. The past is completely forgiven, wiped out. In the world of the chicken, such treatment, such complete acceptance and forgiveness, is not only unexpected, it is incomprehensible and impossible.

However, if we examine forgiveness in a new way, we will be able to see how it worked in the parable and how it works in our own lives. So, let me begin this chapter by giving an overview of forgiveness, after which we will go into the dynamics of the process of forgiveness.

Picture with me a loving Father who walks into his son's room while the sleeping son is having a nightmare. The Father knows that the child is all right but is just having a nightmare. But He also knows that if He were to awaken the child while he is in the nightmare, the child would become more frightened. So the Father decides to send a messenger into his son's dream with the sole purpose of helping the son create a happy and loving dream. When the son recognizes and follows the Father's messenger (the eagle), rather than the source of the nightmare (the chicken), a happy dream begins to gently unfold. Once the happy dream has replaced the nightmare, the Father can awaken the child with no fear.

It is not difficult to look at this situation and discover how it illustrates the dynamics of the eagle and chicken. The child having the nightmare, of course, represents us as we listen to the voice of the chicken, with its emphasis on our guilt and the punishment that we must expect. The messenger sent by the concerned Father (who is clearly God) is present in our lives as the eagle, whose voice it is that constantly and quietly reminds us of the way back home to the Father. And the eagle's message, very simply, is that we are forgiven. There is no need for guilt, there is no punishment in store for us: the Father eagerly awaits our return, and we are forgiven.

This parable, then, shows us forgiveness at work in a symbolic manner. Now, to set the stage for a more in-depth examination of forgiveness, let's go to the movies, our personal movies. Picture yourself sitting in your own personal movie theater. The action you see on the screen is your life as it has happened so far, and all the action and events happening in the present are seen as being real and true. It feels true because, as you watch the film, you experience the mood swings of the movie, from ecstatic happiness to deep despair and depression. It seems so real, in fact, that you feel that you are a victim of whatever is being dramatized on the screen. You experience yourself as powerless, as if someone else (the chicken) were in the projection room deciding what films you need to see, as if someone else were running your life.

After years of looking at these re-runs of your life experiences, you become deeply discouraged. There seems to be no way to find lasting peace and happiness. Though there are moments of joy as you watch the film, the projectionist/chicken always seems to arrange what you see in such a way that the joy soon vanishes, to be replaced by those old, familiar feelings of fear, anger, and guilt. Every event that you see always ends in the same way: with pain, disappointment and suffering. Like the daytime soap operas, no problem is ever really solved.

As you watch and experience these films, you are communicating to yourself what you believe is really the truth about you, that there is something basically wrong with you. You have a fatal flaw, the films seem to say, you must have done something so bad that it can never be forgiven. Inside of you must be some horrible monster, for you to have come to this unhappy situation.

At this point, when you seem to have nowhere left to turn, from deep within, you hear that still small voice (the eagle) saying, "There is another set of films, there is another way to see yourself and the world." Suddenly, there is a moment of remembering, as if some ancient memory is being heard. Out of your pain and frustration, you open yourself to hearing the message of possibility brought by this voice. You feel as if a messenger has been sent to you with some good news, and you hunger to hear his words, see his films.

"There is another way to look at these events on the screen," the voice repeats. "You are not a victim of what's on the screen. You were the one who originally invited the chicken to run your show; you have chosen to sit in your theater seat acting as if you had nothing to do with the movies you watched. But you are not powerless: there is another choice — the eagle — and your power lies in being able to make that choice. You yourself are in the projection room in charge of the films you see, and up till now you have only been seeing the chicken's films."

Now you can begin to notice that there is another set of films, and these have been produced by the eagle. Eagerly, you put a reel of the eagle's film on the projector, and you watch as it begins to play. At first, it seems puzzling, because you are seeing the same events as before. But soon you realize that something is very different. This time, as you watch, you experience power and freedom, and there are no feelings of depression and despair such as you felt before. You sense peace inside. The old truth you believed to be true about yourself seems to be fading in this new Light. Joyfully, you begin to see the real Truth: you are Love, Peace, Joy, Freedom, and Light.

The process of forgiveness cannot begin until we reach the point illustrated in our imaginary projection room: that moment of recognition that we are the source of our own experience and that we have the choice of how we will see ourselves, another person, or an event: through the eyes of the chicken or the eyes of the eagle. Our power is in the choosing: *we decide* whether to choose the film of the chicken and see the experiences of our lives through feelings of fear or to choose the film of the eagle and see those same experiences through feelings of love and forgiveness. The power is in the choice, as is vividly illustrated by the picture on the following page.

* * *

CHOICE
CHICKEN FILM
?
EAGLE FILM
BEVERLY LITTON

CHAPTER 6

THE UNDOING

With the above scenario in mind, let us begin to look at the eagle's way of undoing the chicken's philosophy through the dynamics of forgiveness.

The first step in forgiveness is to bring the problem back to its source. Remember, the chicken keeps telling us to deny our guilt, and fear, and to project it on someone or something else outside of ourselves, to consider that other person or thing as the real problem. We are supposed to believe that this is the only way we can protect ourselves from what we think is the real truth about ourselves, that we are sinners, that something is basically wrong with us, and that we will have to face an angry god who waits for his pound of flesh. All of this makes us extremely fearful, and this is why this first step seems so difficult.

The eagle simply says, "Let us bring the cause of our problems back to its true source — our own mind." In other words, he asks us to realize that we are the ones running the projector, and thus we are creating our own inner experiences. He wants us to accept the responsibility for choosing to put the films of the chicken on our projector, for deciding to respond with anger or fear to the situations and people we encounter in our lives. Though this is perhaps the most difficult moment in the whole process, it is only as we become willing to take this step, to see things in this way, that we will ever be able to see that there is another way, the eagle's way.

When people come to me as a psychotherapist, they are always stuck in the chicken's system of thought. Fear, anger, and guilt rule their lives, and yet they continue to behave as they have always behaved, following the same patterns over and over. Even when they know their actions will merely create more pain, they continue to step to the same drum. The chicken's system has become so familiar, and besides, there just doesn't seem to be any other way.

For example, one lady with whom I was working was going through a divorce. In our early sessions together, she was full of anger, relating a number of experiences which had occurred during her marriage, experiences which she had reacted to with a great deal of anger and pain at the time, and which continued to arouse those same feelings in her. She was, all in all, a very unhappy woman.

However, as we worked together, she began to be aware of how, in many of these situations, she had expected her husband to behave a certain way, to be a certain kind of person, so that she could feel secure. When he didn't meet the expectations she had set for him in her mind, she would become angry at him and fearful for herself, feeling insecure and vulnerable. And then it began to dawn on her that, by behaving this way, she had really been refusing to take the responsibility for her own life.

I wish I could say that once she reached this awareness, there was a wonderful blast of trumpets, a chorus of angel voices sang "The Halleluia Chorus," and she walked out of my office and lived happily ever after. Not at all. What happened was that she had very mixed feelings. On the one hand, if she accepted that she had been the source of her unpleasant experiences and feelings in this relationship and had had a part in creating the mess, she knew she would have to face her own internal fear, anger, guilt, and inadequacy. At this point, she felt totally powerless to deal with all of that. But, on the other hand, she sensed that, as soon as she was able to face these fears, there was another possibility available to her, another way of looking at the situation that would not lead her in the old frustrating direction.

Her choice was not at all an easy one, but she soon learned that every time she chose to accept the responsibility for creating her own experience, she felt a little more power within herself, and it became a little easier to choose that direction when the next situation arose. In other words, this first step in the process of forgiveness is, itself, a process — one of moving back and forth between the fear threatened by the chicken and the possibility held out by the eagle. If we are willing to press on, we will find the feeling that we have the power to choose becoming stronger and stronger, until we can and do accept that we truly are the ones in the projection rooms, choosing the films we will see.

So, simply stated, the first step is to bring the cause of our problems back to its source, our own minds, and accept that we are the ones projecting and thus creating our own internal experiences. It sounds simple — and it is. But it's not easy.

Once we are willing to take this first step, the eagle can now show us how we can use the very heart of the chicken's program, projection (with which we have become so familiar), and turn it into the very tool by which we heal our own minds. If we are willing to accept that what was on the screen was created by choice, then, when we change our minds and decide to put on the eagle's film, a transformation occurs. The screen on which we are projecting our film becomes a mirror. Instead of merely watching our life experiences occur "out there," those situations are now reflected back to us to show us what needs healing within ourselves.

As this transformation from movie screen to mirror occurs, the eagle suggests a very powerful and helpful principle by which we can benefit from the change. As we look into the mirror, he says, we should begin to see every event, every situation, and every person as our teacher. Rather than reacting with those old familiar responses of anger or irritation or disappointment, we need to look again and ask ourselves what we can learn. Let me give you several examples of what is meant by this.

If you happen to live in a large city where traffic is a problem, you will appreciate this first example. Picture yourself on your way through city traffic to a very important meeting. As is your custom, you have left yourself a little extra time for potential traffic problems, but you are suddenly dismayed to find that traffic has come to a complete stop, and it appears that you won't be moving for a while. You immediately begin to worry: what will people say when you get to your destination? More importantly, what will they think? Will you lose any chance of achieving the goal you had set for the meeting?

As your fear grows, it begins to be accompanied by outward signs of your impatience: you begin to honk your horn, you start yelling at the cars in front of you, you (and your car) start to overheat, and you can feel yourself starting to sweat. You have let your colleagues down: you promised to be at that meeting, and now you won't be — or you'll be very late. In a very brief moment, your mind has become filled with thoughts of fear, anger, and guilt. Who — or what — has caused all these unpleasant feelings in your mind? Why, the traffic jam, obviously. It certainly wasn't your fault that you got caught in it — you were simply an innocent victim. What you are having at this moment is a chicken attack.

Suddenly, you remember what you have been learning, and you realize that you have been looking at this situation through the chicken's film. The clues are obvious: you feel fearful, angry, very unhappy and uncomfortable, and you are putting the blame on something outside of your own mind: you are feeling like a victim in the situation. It is a simple matter for you to choose to put away the chicken's film, and instead view the situation through the eagle's film. The eagle's film is put on your inner projector through the process of forgiveness, which will be discussed in the next chapter.

Now you see the situation around you from the eagle's perception. The traffic jam was not "arranged" in order to make you late; it is simply the way things are going at this moment. The eagle reminds you that *you* are in charge of this minute, and you can put it to whatever use you wish. You could pick up the newspaper lying on the seat next to you and spend a few minutes reading; you could pull out the cassette tape you have been intending to listen to; or you could simply sit in quiet thought. You could not have anticipated the traffic problem, and you are not responsible for it.; but, as you feel yourself cooling off and quieting down, you realize that it has been a benefit to you by providing you with the opportunity to practice the steps of forgiveness. Because you allowed the experience to mirror you back to yourself, rather than giving it the power to determine for you how you would react to it, you have learned a little bit more of the eagle's way. A potentially unpleasant situation has become your teacher.

Let's look at another, more serious situation. Eighteen years ago, when I was in the parish ministry, I went through a divorce, and at that time, divorced ministers were not in demand. Not only was my marriage going down the tubes, but so was my career; in fact, I felt I was almost literally going down the tube. I'm sure it's not hard to imagine the fear, the guilt, the frustration and anger that filled my mind most of my days and nights.

At this time, I was getting help from a therapist, and he had been listening to me over a period of weeks become more and more discouraged and frustrated. There finally came a day when it looked to me as if things couldn't possibly get worse, and I had really reached the end of my resources. "This is really tragic," I told him. I'll never forget what he said to me in response to that statement.

"Jerry," he said calmly, "what you're experiencing is not a tragedy." Seeing my confused response, he went on to explain, "The events of life are neutral. The tragedy comes when you allow the events of life to stop you from continuing to fulfill the person you were created to be and you start dying. That's tragedy.

"Now," he continued, "there are two events in your life right now: your divorce and your career. You can either sit here and wallow in them, or you can go *through* them, learn from them, grow from them, and come out on the other end a more open, honest, and aware person. It's your choice."

This was a turning point in my life. I could either see myself as a victim or I could take charge of myself and make some different choices. To put it in the terms of this book, I could keep running the film of the chicken, or I could ask for the eagle's help, put on his film, and, using the events as a mirror, begin to see what needed to be healed and corrected in my relationships and in my life. Again, it was a simple choice — but I certainly don't want to give the impression that it was easy.

In fact, it is downright difficult to break our old familiar habits of reacting with anger or fear to situations in which it seems that other people are attacking us. To look in the mirror the eagle holds up for us and see another person as our teacher, when we formerly regarded that person as our enemy, probably seems next to impossible, but my last example vividly illustrates exactly how this can work for us.

Some time ago, I was conducting a seven-week workshop on parent-child communications for a group of parents. For more than six of those seven weeks, one particular lady had become more and more of a problem. She had begun by talking a great deal, and by this time she seemed to dominate most of each meeting. It had taken all of my skill just to set limits on her so that others could also share. It had also become obvious that she was just as irritated with me as I was with her.

During the final session, I was planning to leave early and let my co-therapist finish up. But as I was standing up to go, this woman turned to me and said, "Wait a minute, I've got something I want to tell you."

With fire in her eyes, she went on, "You are the most egotistical, self-centered, conceited person I have ever met, and this workshop has been a waste of my time."

I thought for a moment and then decided to be honest with her. "Well, you have been a real pain to me, too." Then came one of those moments of enlightenment when the spirit within comes through, providing just the right words. I went on, "Do you realize that, at this moment, you and I are friends and are teachers to each other?"

"I don't understand what you're talking about."

"Well," I explained, "there is something about you that really bothers me, and I get upset and angry about it. But if I stop and take a look at this anger inside me, seek to find out what button inside of me got pushed, and then learn from it and grow from it, you have been a blessing to me — and you have also been my teacher. And if you, in turn, do the same thing, try to find out what it is about me that really pushes angry buttons inside of you, then you, too, have the opportunity to learn and grow. So I have been a blessing to you and have been your teacher."

I don't know how she felt about what I said when she had cooled down, but that wasn't what was important. The important thing was that I had stopped and faced the irritation that had been building in me over those weeks, and by sharing my feelings with her, I had made myself see the situation in quite a different way. Instead of leaving the workshop with feelings of anger and frustration, I felt relaxed and at peace. I could bless that lady in my mind, for she had truly been my teacher.

These three examples illustrate in different ways how the eagle takes the same events that the chicken has been using to evoke unpleasant feelings in us, and asks us to choose a different way of seeing them. He asks us to recognize that we are in control of our reactions to the experiences that confront us: if we continue to feel the anger or fear or guilt, it is only because we have chosen to look at the chicken's film. We always have the choice to look at the situation through the eagle's eyes, to see the events and people as opportunities to discover what needs to be healed and forgiven within our own minds at that moment.

As we practice choosing the eagle's film, an interesting thing begins to happen. Whereas before we were perceiving our fears, angers, and guilts as emotions to be denied and avoided,that is no longer true. Through the steps of forgiveness, we are now willing to bring our darkness into the light, and as we watch, the darkness begins to disappear. We look at those feelings of fear, anger, and guilt now as our good friends, because they show us that we are not where we want to be, at peace. They have become in effect, red flags that get our attention, so that we can make another choice, put on the eagle's film, and find more and more often the peace we search for. We are truly on the path Home.

CHAPTER 7

THE STEPS OF FORGIVENESS

We have been discussing the process which leads from projection to forgiveness. Now let us look at the practical steps that we can take and practice at any moment when we become aware that the chicken film is running. As we look closely at each of these four steps, we can reach an even greater awareness of how the process can work in our lives.

STEP I
BRING THE PROBLEM BACK TO THE SOURCE

The first step is to acknowledge that our experience of fear, anger, guilt does not come from outside ourselves. Rather, we are the source of every experience we have. If we feel anger (or any other feeling, pleasant or unpleasant), *we* created it in ourslves as our chosen response to some person or event. The **Course in Miracles** puts this idea in a beautiful way:

> ***"I am responsible for what I see.***
> ***I choose the feelings I experience, and decide upon the goal I would achieve.***
> ***And everything that seems to happen to me I ask for, and receive as I have asked."*** [11]

---

[11] **Course in Miracles,** Text, p. 418. Foundation for Inner Peace, Box 635, Tiburon, California 94920.

This initial phase of the forgiveness process, then, requires that you own your own feelings, experiences and problems, and acknowledge them to yourself. At the moment of fear, anger, guilt, confusion, anxiety, etc., declare to yourself, "I am the source of what I am experiencing at this moment. I am choosing to look at this person or situation through the eyes of fear." By realizing this, you bring the problem back to the place — your mind — where you can make another choice, put another film on the projector, a film that allows you to see the moment through the eyes of the eagle.

A simple affirmation can illustrate this first step of bringing the problem back to its source: "I forgive you for not being the way I wanted you to be. I take back my projection and let you go."

STEP II
LOOK AT THE FEAR, ANGER, OR GUILT

Before we can say yes, we must say no, or, more appropriately in this case, before we can truly release these feelings, we must accept them as ours. When we have made the decision to own our feelings, it is important to let ourselves actually feel them. This second step, then, asks us to experience what happens inside of us when we acknowledge that we made ourselves angry or fearful or guilty. So many people want to bypass this step because it seems so painful. But it is important to let the feelings come up into the light if we want that light to shine them away.

Now, this does not mean that you sit and wallow in these feelings, letting the whole world know just how angry or fearful or guilty you are. Instead, this means to let yourself become conscious of them, experience them, as a reminder that this is not what you would choose to have in your experience. In other words, you are able to see clearly what you don't want to do and to feel and to be, and you can now make the choice to say "No" to the chicken's way of perception.

The pamphlet, **Psychotherapy: Purpose, Process and Practice**, has a clear way of describing this step.

> *Healing occurs as a patient begins to hear the dirge he sings, and questions its validity. Until he hears it, he cannot understand that it is he who sings it to himself. To hear it is the first step to recovery. To question it must then become his choice.*
>
> *There is a tendency, and it is very strong, to hear this song of death only an instant, and then dismiss it uncorrected. These floating awarenesses represent the many opportunities given us literally "to change our tune." The sound of healing can be heard instead. But first the willingness to question the "truth" of the song of condemnation must arise.*[12]

In this second step, it is necessary to hear this dirge we are singing to ourselves at the moment when we are singing it, so that we can say "No" to it. Thus, we become open to seeing the person or

---

[12] **Psychotherapy: Purpose, Process and Practice**, p. 12, Foundation for Inner Peace, Box 635, Tiburon, California, 94920.

situation differently. Saying "No" to this dirge moves us toward that power, the eagle, that can transform the moment.

STEP III
ASK FOR HELP

Once you have allowed yourself to experience this fear, anger or guilt, once you have realized that you are looking at a person or situation from the chicken's point of view and have made the decision to see things differently, the next step is to ask the eagle, who is always within you, to help you see this person or situation through the eyes of love. In other words, you simply ask for help. There are no magic words by which you do this, there is no special ritual; the only thing necessary is that you be *truly willing* to see the moment differently. If you are not willing to change your mind, to look at the situation from a different perspective, your words will have no power. The words in your mind must be the expression of your heart's desire in that moment.

STEP IV
LET THE EAGLE DO THE WORK

Now comes the really good news. We only need to have the willingness to take the first three steps. Then our part is over, and in that moment, the eagle within us will take away our guilt and fear. This experience is not new to any of us. We can all remember a time when we were in a state of confusion or anxiety or fear; we asked for help, and fifteen minutes later, we noticed we were feeling more peaceful. This is exactly what happens in this final step in the process: we make the choice of the film we want to watch, and the eagle does the rest.

But, just in case you are thinking that there is some kind of magic involved here, let me caution you about this process. It takes willingness and practice to make these steps work for you. Remember, you have believed what the chicken has told you about yourself, it has seemed to be the truth for a long time, until it has become a habit to think of yourself in that way. To change that habit, you must be willing to bring your fears, angers, and guilts into your own awareness. Then you can make another choice.

Also, you must keep in mind that change only takes place in the moment, nowhere else. Every moment you are aware of confusion, anxiety, guilt, fear, anger, is an opportunity to go through these steps. As you practice forgiveness in that moment, that moment is changed. Not the next moment, just that moment. Each moment is a new opportunity to put on the eagle's film. You will hit the mark and miss it, hit it and miss it, hit it, hit it, hit it, miss it, etc. Eventually, change becomes the accumulation of all of those changed moments. Thus, the more you can become aware of your moments of fear, guilt, depression, etc., the more opportunities you will have to choose once again, asking the eagle to put on his film of love.

CHAPTER 8

THE EXPERIENCE OF PRACTICING FORGIVENESS

Once we have made the choice to see things differently, to practice forgiveness, we are at the point at which the unfolding process of forgiveness begins. But almost before we can take a good strong step along this new path, we encounter the first of several difficulties that are likely to arise, and in this section, I would like to point out these difficulties so that we can be ready for them.

Remember, we have decided to reject the chicken's way, which he realizes, quite correctly, is his undoing. He immediately tries to get us back in line with tactics that range from suspiciousness to viciousness. The more determined we are to practice forgiveness, the more vicious he will become. He will push every fear, anger, and guilt button we have — and some we didn't even know we had. As I tell my patients, it will get worse before it gets better, but if we are prepared for what is ahead, it will get better.

Let me use an analogy here. Picture yourself in a house in which you have lived for many years. During these years, you have been operating within the chicken's way of life, and one result of this is that, instead of taking your garbage out of the house and getting rid of it, you have been stuffing it into your closets. When the closets were full, you looked around and found empty rooms you weren't using and began to fill them up, one after another, with garbage. There's a lot of smell to deal with, and you do begin to wonder where you're going to put the garbage when you run out of empty rooms, but you look around at your neighbors and see that they're doing the same thing, so you figure you'll find a solution someday.

This analogy is very apt, for our minds are, in many ways, where we live, the "houses" we inhabit every waking — and sleeping — moment, and the fear thoughts, the anger, the pain that so often take up residence in there with us are the "garbage" of our minds, the refuse, the stuff which ought to be thrown out. But, just as in the analogy, we don't throw out our garbage. We put it back in some dark closet and shut the door on it — and maybe we even fool ourselves that it's no longer there.

But all of a sudden, something will be said or done, that door will open, and that awful, smelly mess will come tumbling out of the closet, right into the "living rooms" of our minds. There will be that anger or guilt or fear, just as "fresh" as the day we stuffed it in that closet — probably "fresher"! It is no wonder that we can sometimes reach the point mentally that the prodigal son in the parable reached literally: we feel we can sink no lower, things can't get any worse — we are living with the pigs.

Let's return to the analogy for a moment. There comes a point when you have had enough of living surrounded by garbage, you decide to do something about it. At first, you clean up just one corner of one room, but something interesting happens almost immediately. With just that one clean area, you have created a contrast: the small clean place stands out even more because it is in such contrast to every other place in your house. Its attractiveness is even greater. Whereas before, your garbage was just garbage with a little "g," now suddenly you see it as Garbage with a capital "G." And you have even greater inspiration to dig out the garbage in your house, and clean the place up.

It is the same in the "houses" of our minds. If we take just one area of our lives that is filled with anger or pain or fear, and have the willingness to own it, to accept that we have been denying it, to bring it into the light, to throw out that way of thinking and reacting, to clean out that closet, the peace that will result in that area will, by contrast, point up all the more clearly how miserable we are when we move back into another of the old messy areas. When we begin to practice forgiveness, it is as if we have turned on a tiny light that instantly shows us how dark it has been. If we continue in this path, asking the eagle for his help, the light will gently increase, gradually doing away with the darkness we have been living in.

Again, the **Course in Miracles** describes this well. "Prisoners bound with heavy chains for years," it says, "starved and emaciated, weak and exhausted, and with eyes so long cast down in darkness they remember not the light, do not leap up in joy the instant they are made free. It takes a while for them to understand what freedom is."[13]

---

[13] Course in Miracles, **Text**, pp. 401-402.

I once had a friend who was chaplain at a mental hospital where I was part of a class of trainees. On our first day on the wards, the chaplain sent us into the wards where the most severely disturbed people were kept. At the conference later that afternoon, we were each asked to share our experiences with the other trainees. One of the students was visibly shaken and explained that he had tried to tell the patients about his particular form of religion, hoping to offer them some comfort in their mental pain and anguish. The patients either completely ignored him or told him outright where he could go, and he just couldn't understand their refusal to be helped.

Tommy, my chaplain friend, had a very wise explanation, using an analogy from Plato. "These people here and many others you will work with are, in a sense, way back in a cave. Now Jesus would not stand at the entrance of that cave and shout down into its depths, 'Hey, you people just come on out of this cave, ok?' No, Jesus goes down into the cave, into the darkness where those people are living, and He slowly and gently helps them come up out of that darkness and into the light of Truth."

That is the eagle's way, too. He helps us to shine the light, little by little, into the closets of our minds that have been full of unhappiness and pain, shining the light more and more deeply into that darkness as time goes on. As often as we are ready to ask for his help, to bring our garbage to him, he is there to aid us in shining away more and more of the garbage we have stored there.

Another of the pitfalls that we need to be on the lookout for is a result of this first one. As we practice forgiveness and see the little areas of light that are beginning to show up in our lives, we can become impatient. We want that peace and joy and happiness now in all the areas of our minds. Our impatience comes from the recognition that, where we thought our house was half full of garbage, we now sense that it's everywhere, filling every room clear to the ceilings. Inside, it feels that we are getting worse, losing ground, slipping back.

But the truth is that, as we clean one corner of a room of its garbage, we create a contrast. There is garbage, as before, but now there is "clean." Because we now have a contrast, our garbage (that fear, anger, and guilt) will look and feel worse than before. It is not really worse; rather, we are beginning to allow ourselves to see and feel the real results (the pain and suffering) of following the chicken's philosophy.

Before long, we will find ourselves feeling better. But feeling better can trap us into thinking we have all the garbage cleaned out. Then, when our fear, anger, or guilt button is punched, we feel that we aren't getting anywhere. And so we go back and forth, vacillating between feeling successful and feeling defeated. This is a normal part of the process.

In fact, it may be helpful, at this point, to describe some of the quite normal emotions and feelings that people new to the practice of forgiveness might experience. Beginners and long-time practitioners must expect to move between some or all of these states — and perhaps even others not mentioned here — as they work at making forgiveness part of every moment of their days.[14]

1. *Feeling disoriented: You may experience yourself as not being grounded, feeling spacey, as if you were not fully present.*

2. *Feeling a sense of seeming terror and panic: It seems as if your world is falling apart. In reality, the world you have created using the chicken's way of thinking is being challenged.*

3. *Feeling that there is no way you can win: This is quite true, because winning and losing are aspects of the chicken's philosophy. In the eagle's way, it is not a case of winning or losing but of loving.*

4. *Feeling as if you were going crazy: The truth is that you are experiencing the results of operating in an insane system.*

5. *Feeling shaky inside: The process of forgiveness is truly a shaking-up of the foundations upon which your life has been based up till now.*

6. *Feeling sadness, perhaps even suddenly finding yourself crying: This, too, is normal for the process. You are releasing some of the pain that has been internalized.*

7. *Feeling a sense of hopelessness, that it will never work: That is only the voice of the chicken saying, "Oh, here we go again. See, I told you this forgiveness stuff doesn't work."*

[14] See **From a Chicken to an Eagle**, p. 47, which is the section on the whirlpool, to supplement what is being discussed here.

Understanding that emotional states such as these are common to the process of moving from the chicken's world to the eagle's world helps us to be prepared, to recognize situations that may be quite upsetting as actually a normal part of the process. We must remind ourselves that we are OK and that these are really signs that we are letting go of more of our guilt.

Kenneth Wapnick, in **Christian Psychology and the Course in Miracles**, has quite clearly summarized this whole process and the difficulties that arise as follows:

> *The obstacle of love is fear, and so fear must be transcended if love is to be accepted as our only reality. We must recognize a problem before it can be solved. To look at fear and guilt is frightening by definition and also by experience. As we continue to progress in the spiritual life, however, we will be increasingly confronted with painful situations. At times we may even experience an increased sense of hopelessness. That is because we are coming nearer to those deeper, more repressed areas of guilt and fear, and the ego screams, "Stop. Go no further." This is the Course's view of the "dark night of the soul," the period of greatest aridity that precedes the final experience of union with God.*
>
> *In desperation the ego attempts to ward off this final step in its undoing, and in its "last ditch stand," seeks to attack us as it never had before. It is at this point that the full terror of our guilt stands exposed, and the temptation to pull back and return to the ego's "comfort" becomes the strongest.*[15]

---

[15] **Christian Psychology and the Course in Miracles**, p. 16, Foundation for the Course in Miracles, Box 783, Crompond, NY 10517.

One other factor must be remembered when we are in the midst of these unsettling periods: very often, we will not be functioning at 100% awareness. In fact, our awareness may sometimes drop as low as 50%. For example, you might be driving to work and suddenly begin to cry or feel angry. When such intense feeling unexpectedly overwhelms you, obviously your awareness of whatever you might be doing will drop drastically. I found myself in just this situation, and I almost hit the car in front of me. When I recovered control of my own car, I realized I was having a chicken attack and my awareness of what I was doing was much lower than it should have been. So I put an extra car length between myself and the car in front of me. In this way, I compensated for that lessened attention. And this is my suggestion to others who are in the midst of these periods. Do not deny the experience, but rather accept it, and then compensate for it. Thus, it does not need to run your show.

More importantly, as you go through these experiences, continue to practice the forgiveness process, asking for the eagle's help. Being persistent in practicing forgiveness is one of the major elements of the process. Remember the story of the snail who, one bitter cold morning in January, started to climb the frozen trunk of a cherry tree. As he slowly moved upward, a beetle stuck his head out of a crack in the tree and said, "Hey, buddy, you're wasting your time. There aren't any cherries up there." The snail kept right on going but turned to the beetle, saying, "There will be when I get there."

Being persistent in practicing forgiveness does pay off, but usually not in a dramatic way. As we practice, we begin to see results in little surprises that will start to pop up here and there in our everyday experiences. One day, out of the blue, we'll realize, "You know, I was in my boss's office today, and he was all upset as usual, but I didn't react the way I used to. I stayed calm for a change."

Or perhaps we'll hear, "I couldn't believe what just popped out of my mouth when she asked me to help on that committee next month. I said 'No,' that I was already doing all I could handle. And she wasn't upset, and I feel great!"

Or maybe even, "Someone really disappointed me the other day — if that had happened two months ago, I would have gone to pieces. But now, I realize that I'm handling it; my life is moving ahead, and I'm even happy now and then. Amazing!"

What we need to realize as we practice forgiveness is that, unlike the instant credit that is so prevalent in our society, where we have whatever we want now and pay for it later, we must practice first. The results will come, not in a flash, with fanfares and fireworks, but slowly and steadily over time.

And this leads us directly to the third pitfall we must be aware of simply because, in a process like this, we don't change overnight, we can grow discouraged and weary, feeling that we will be working at it forever. After a while, what should be a source of more and more joy in our lives becomes a burden which we think we will never be rid of. But, by now, we should easily recognize the chicken's voice in those words; such ideas are exactly what the he hopes to push into our minds, replacing Truth with his old ideas.

We need to remember that, as novices, learners, we are like fledgling pianists. No one ever sat down at a piano and was instantly able to perform like Horowitz or Liberace. There must always be a period of watching the keys, learning the notes, working at scales. Gradually the learner begins to feel at home and comfortable at the keyboard, and only then is there a sense of flow, so that the music begins to come seemingly without effort.

Similarly, we need to realize that, though it seems tedious at first, the more we practice our new ways, the more easily we will move toward the point where, whenever we feel fear, anger, guilt, confusion, or any other unpleasantness, we will automatically recognize that once again we have the chance to choose whose films we will watch. Sooner than we realize, our efforts and practicing will pay off, and it will become habit to choose the eagle's film.

There is a more extensive discussion of this process, its difficulties and its rewards, in the second part of my book, **From a Chicken to an Eagle**, which can help to supplement what is described above. For now, though, we must understand that forgiveness is simple but not easy. As we practice forgiveness, we are beginning to change the very basis of what we think is true about ourselves and the world. Perhaps it will help you to understand this if I give you an illustration of what it means to really forgive and how it is a process.

Several years ago, in a midwest city, a young teenage boy raped and killed a young girl. The parents of the boy disowned him and left him to the mercy of the courts. He was convicted and sent to prison. A surprising thing then happened. After the boy had been in prison for several months, the girl's parents began to visit him, and these visitations continued until the boy was released on parole. When he was released, the girl's parents took this boy into their home and accepted him as their son.

Notice in this illustration that the parents of the dead girl did not immediately move towards the boy who had killed their daughter. They had to work through their own pain and suffering in the loss of their child. But, in the hearts of these two people, there was an openness to forgiveness. The first few visits they made to the boy in prison must have been very difficult for them, but they were persistent. Their willingness to continue the process of forgiveness transformed the way they saw this boy.

Before we move on to examine love as we find it in the chicken's system and then in the eagle's, let us again review the steps of forgiveness.

Step 1: *I recognize that you are not my enemy or the source of my problems. I have created the world of my experience.*

Step 2: *I am willing to see that the chicken's way is a path I have chosen, a path which has only produced constant fear, anger, and guilt. Now I can make another choice.*

Step 3: *I choose the Eagle. I ask for His help to see the situation differently, through His eyes of love.*

Step 4: *The Eagle takes away the fear, anger, and guilt. Now I can experience who I really am, a child of love and peace, and I see clearly that you are not my enemy but are my brother or sister in love.*

We can now see clearly that the more we practice forgiveness, the more the eagle can change the way we see ourselves and our brother.

CHICKEN FILM

EAGLE FILM

FORGIVENESS

PART III

LOVE

THROUGH THE EYES OF THE CHICKEN

THROUGH THE EYES OF THE EAGLE

CHAPTER 9

THE CHICKEN'S WAY OF LOVE

By now, you have become familiar with the contrasting dynamics of the philosophies of the chicken and the eagle, as well as the steps we must take to move from the former to the latter. And you have also learned about the process of forgiveness, around which the eagle's philosophy revolves. You probably understand, too, that love is the foundation of forgiveness, which, when practiced, moves us from guilt, anger, and fear to love and peace. But perhaps you are feeling a bit confused at this point.

After all, though you may recognize that you have been following the chicken's philosophy up to this point, you know that your life has not been without love. More than likely, you have experienced a great deal of love of many different kinds, love for a parent, love for a spouse, love for a child, love for a friend, love for a pet, even love for a car or house or other object. Why hasn't the love that has been part of your life until now been enough to bring you the happiness you have sought?

To answer this question, we need to go back and examine each philosophy in greater depth to discover just where the differences lie. In the first part of this section, we will use two familiar images to give a broad outline of the process that is at work in the chicken's way of love, and we will go on to look in depth at how the chicken's love works in our world. Then, in the second part of this section, we will make a similar study of the eagle's way of love, to show how it differs and how it manifests itself.

To fully understand the chicken's way of love, we must go back to the basic presupposition of the chicken philosophy, which is that we have sinned. Out of this mistaken belief has come a deep conviction that there is something wrong with us. We feel this "something wrong" as a lack, as something missing inside of us, and so we feel we are incomplete. In this way, what we call the "principle of scarcity" comes into operation.

The next step in the process is obvious: wherever there is lack, there is immediately a sense of need. In other words, in the world of the chicken, the "principle of need" always accompanies the scarcity principle. Since we lack something and feel incomplete, then, of course, there is something we need. And it seems just as obvious that if we feel this need for something, it must be because we don't have it, and so we must look elsewhere for it. Remember, too, that there is an even stronger reason for not looking inside of ourselves: we are afraid to deal with the guilt that reminds us of what we have done to God and of the fear of the anticipated punishment.

The third principle at work in the chicken philosophy is the "principle of dependency": if we can only be complete by finding something outside of ourselves to fill our need, then, by implication, we are dependent upon that external something for our completeness. Now, this external object that we are seeking can be almost anything we find in the world around us. It can be something tangible, such as food or money, or intangible, such as power or fame, but very often it takes the form of another person, and this is the situation we will consider in our discussion.

Thus, as we look outside ourselves to meet our needs, we decide we must find a person that we feel will have the capacity to meet these needs. Of course, this will be a special person, so that, when we find this person, we immediately develop a special relationship, unconsciously putting them on a pedestal and seeing them as our source of being OK and complete. And, of course, more often than not, the name that we give to the feeling we have for this person is "love."

But once we have settled on someone who seems to be able to meet our needs, something unconsciously but inevitably happens: we tend no longer to see that person as another complete and independent person, but rather we see only his or her capacity to meet our needs. And, at the same time, this process is going on with the other person, who no longer sees us as we are but rather sees us as meeting his or her needs. Remember, much of this process is unconscious, but it works very smoothly and unobtrusively as we form this special relationship with another.

However, something further is going on, too. As we become more and more dependent on this special other person to meet our needs, as we fall more deeply "in love," that dependency is having some very unpleasant results. We soon learn that to be dependent on something or someone else always creates hostility, and hostility creates guilt, and now we have arrived back at the basic principle and foundation of the chicken system. As we have already seen, the "glue" that holds the chicken philosophy together is made up of fear, anger and guilt, and that glue is exactly what is at work here in special relationships.

Now, this is all a very logical process, even though, as we know, it is based on an absolutely incorrect assumption and leads us directly away from the Truth about ourselves. Once we have decided that we are sinners, the three principles that we have discussed begin to operate without our conscious awareness of what is going on. The diagram on the next page presents a graphic picture of this process.

THE CHICKEN'S WAY OF LOVE

We lack something — we are incomplete.

⇩

Need is created:
we must do something to fill this lack.

⇩

We look outside of ourselves to meet this need

We find a person or thing that we feel
will meet our need.

We create a special relationship:
in effect, we put that person or thing on a pedestal.

Dependency comes as a result of our
special relationship.

Dependency creates hostility.

Hostility leads us back to guilt, the basis of
the chicken system — and the cycle starts all over again.

Diagram 3

Let us look at two illustrations which will further clarify how love works in the chicken's system, especially how we take the step which leads us from dependency on to hostility toward the "loved" one. In the first illustration, we will use the image of a jar to represent the three principles, scarcity, need, and dependency, at work in the chicken's way of love and special relationships.[16]

Figure 6

The jar represents our concept of ourselves, what we really believe to be true about us as a person. Deep within the jar, we find the dark printed word,

[16] The source of this illustration is Dr. Kenneth Wapnick, Director, Foundation for A Course in Miracles.

"GUILT." This represents the feeling we have inside us that we have done something wrong. But, because it is dark and unpleasant to face, we have decided it isn't there. In fact, we think there is nothing there, a big emptiness. And it is this feeling, this lack, that creates in us a sense of needing someone else and sends us out in our search for a special relationship.

We want this other person to fill the lack that we sense deep with us, but, on a deeper level, we need this special relationship to help us avoid facing that dark feeling of guilt that we are afraid to look at, to acknowledge. All of our efforts, including our efforts to find a special relationship, are directed at not allowing those feelings of guilt to come into our conciousness, keeping it always in our unconscious, buried deep within our jar.

So, the lid on the jar represents the other person with whom we have fallen in love. Since the lid prevents us from seeing down into the jar, we think that the problem is solved, that the lack has been filled. This person, then, becomes doubly special to us: first, as the supplier of our need, and second, on an unconscious level, as the barrier that keeps that guilt out of our sight.

With this figure of the jar in mind, let us use a typical dating relationship to present the dynamics of this situation (although, as we will see, those dynamics are at work in any other special relationship, parent-child, friend-friend, boss-employee, husband-wife, etc). Imagine that, in this dating relationship, I have begun dating you, and we seem to be moving toward "falling in love." You grow more and more special to me, and soon you have become the lid on my jar. You are now not only the source of my feeling good about myself but also, because you are a good lid, you are the reason I don't feel any of my guilt. This can be called the "getting together to keep warm" syndrome, because everything you are doing for me, I am doing for you, too. You and I feel wonderful, the lids are tightly on our jars, and everything seems fine.

As time passes and we attempt to meet each other's needs, one of the things I get in the habit of doing is calling you eight times a week. I do this for many weeks; you come to expect the calls, and you are reassured. The quantity of calls now becomes a representation of how much I love you.

Then, inadvertently, one week I call you only six times. At first, you aren't alarmed, but then, the next week, there are again only six calls. This time, you decide that I have begun to move away from you. The lid on your jar begins to unscrew, and that dark mass of guilt at the bottom of the jar starts to rise. You immediately begin asking yourself what's wrong. The relationship no longer feels secure, and your guilt continues to rise.

Because you had come to count on me to behave in a certain way, when my behavior changes, you feel our relationship is threatened. I seem to be the cause of this threat, so, at some point, you will confront me, trying to make me feel guilty for what you think I have done.. "What's wrong with our relationship?" you will ask. "You used to call more often, and now you don't seem to be as interested as you were before. What have I done wrong to cause you to move away?"

Each of these statements creates guilt in me for not being the way you want me to be, so I feel guilty and promise you that everything is OK and that I will go back to calling you eight times a week once again. The lid screws back tightly on your jar.

As might be expected, however, I feel attacked by you, and even though I may comply with your wishes, I unconsciously want to attack you back. But because of my own fear of disturbing the contents of my own jar, I don't. Now, though, you are more sensitive to my actions, and you begin to distrust me and to find other places where I seem to be backing away (thus causing the lid of your jar to unscrew a little more). You find ways to ask in one way or another why I don't behave the way I used to. Feeling attacked again, I attack back by only calling you five times a week.

Your fear weakens the specialness of our relationship, and so the lid unscrews on my jar; my subtle attacks act in the same way to unscrew the lid on your jar. This process can go on for months or years; at any rate, it continues until one of us becomes tired of the game and decides to break off the relationship.

Of course, this means that there is no longer someone out there to fill our need, to keep the lid screwed tightly on our jar, so the guilt we have been trying for so long to avoid begins to surface. Now we are in a panic: if we don't do something, we will have to face that terrible sinner within us. Obviously, we must go out and find someone else to be the lid on our jar.

As we mentioned earlier, this process occurs in most of our relationships with other people, especially with those close to us, and can also happen in relationships we have with objects in our lives, such as jobs, cars, clothes, status, power, and so forth. In other words, anyone or anything that will give us a sense of security can function as the lid of our jar. Figures 7—11present this process in picture form:

Figure 7

Figure 8

Figure 9

If the source of our security, the lid on our jar, leaves us, the guilt pops into our consciousness, and we feel fear and panic. We are no longer secure.

GUILT

Figure 10

Figure 11

Here, let's look at another illustration of how the chicken's way of love works. To do this, we can still use our dating illustration. As before, then, let's assume that I am hoping to find a special relationship in order to fill the emptiness and loneliness I have felt in my life. One day, I notice you, become interested, and decide to ask you for a date so that I can get to know you. As it happens, you are also looking for someone to fill a lack in your life, so you agree to a date.

This initial contact proves to be interesting, and we follow it with a second and a third date. As we spend more and more time together, I begin telling you how wonderful you are and that just being in your presence makes me feel so good. What I am really doing is putting my security eggs in your basket. In return, you are telling me how wonderful I am, that I make you feel accepted and comfortable, and that you think about me all the time. You are now putting your security eggs in my basket. For a while, our experience of each other is very intense and wonderful, and our being together seems like the answer that we have been seeking forever. Our lives have become centered on each other; everything else in our world falls away, and there is just you and me riding off into the sunset.

As we each begin to nurture the hope that the inner lack and incompleteness we feel will be filled by the other, we are really giving up the control of our own lives. I have put my security eggs in your basket, to give you the responsibility for my happiness and well-being. And, for your part, you are putting your security eggs in my basket, making me the source of your feelings of being okay, of being loved and accepted.

And the moment we each put our security eggs in the other's basket, we become enemies. By making you responsible for my happiness, I have given you the power over my sense of self-worth. You are now my enemy because you are in charge of my well-being. You have my security eggs and can jump up and down on them or, even worse, run off with them. And, of course, I can do the same with yours.

Clearly, then, we must both be on our guard constantly. Since you are now my source of self-worth, I must be sure you never leave me or even give a hint of not being there. Our relationship is now based on fear; we are together not for the joy of being with each other, but rather because we can't face the emptiness that would result if the other were to leave. Do you remember that "getting together to keep warm" syndrome we mentioned earlier in this chapter? Here we have the classic case.

After a while, this "getting together to keep warm," which started off as such a wonderful, happy time, becomes stagnant and sterile. The reason for this is clear. Neither of us is free to be ourselves, to be spontaneous and natural. We must maintain the posture that first "hooked" our partner, or else we will each be responsible for the other's distress and pain. And so, we become bored, lifeless, and unhappy, and we begin accusing each other of withholding what is needed to feel alive.

"If you would just do this or be that, I wouldn't feel so empty," we complain. "It's all your fault that I'm not happy. I thought you told me you would make me happy." Statements like these push our guilt buttons, and we fall back into line trying to please the other person. We aren't able to see that our relationship is held together, not by love but by fear and guilt.

One day I notice you are looking at someone else very intensely. My fear button is punched; my fear feelings tell me you are attracted to that person — who must have something I don't have — and you probably will leave me, taking with you, of course, my eggs. Panic begins to set in and my only alternative is to bring you back in line.

"I saw the way you were looking at that person. There must be something wrong with me and our relationship. Maybe you don't love me anymore." Feeling attacked and guilty, you begin defending yourself and at the same time trying to reassure me that everything is all right. The situation levels out, and we go on keeping warm. But we feel even more trapped — with each of us clinging to the other, unable to let go — and we are still bored.

But our existence continues. For a while, because we want to keep the peace and not create any problems, we keep quiet. But, inevitably, this precarious balance cannot be maintained. I begin to stay at the office an extra hour or two each evening. Some time passes before you notice this pattern of spending less time with you. But when you do notice, your fear button is punched. Once again, concern that I will move away from you — thus taking away from you your precious security eggs — conjures up pictures of being left alone, abandonment, and alienation.

"I've noticed you're staying away from me," you complain. "I guess you don't love me anymore. Your job is more important than I am. Maybe you ought to just stay at your office. I feel like you are just using me anyway." I begin feeling guilty and attacked and try to reassure you that it's just temporary, and that I do love you and will spend more time at home. Once more, a sense of relief comes over the relationship — not peace but relief. We have now reached the point where our relationship is a mechanical success but an emotional failure.

If either one of our fear levels becomes too high, threatening to upset this false balance of our lives, we can use the ultimate weapon, the ace in the hole: "I'm just going to leave." This statement strikes terror to our very core. For either one of us to pull out of the situation means the other would lose the source of his or her security and well-being. The feeling is like a death sentence.

So we may continue to stay together for a period of time, but what is holding us together — the glue of our relationship — is fear, anger and guilt. We are trying to create a loving relationship, but it is based on fear, and the only outcome possible is the destruction of the relationship. Thus, we see that, in the chicken philosophy, any relationship we have with people or objects outside of ourselves has its source and sustaining power in fear, anger and guilt.[17]

Here, let me make some general comments about the chicken's way of love or special relationships. It is clear that special relationships operating according to the chicken may seem to be based on love but actually only thinly cover feelings of hate. Remember, the chicken is helping us to hide our guilt from ourselves because it is a reminder of how bad we think we are. The very fact that I need you is an indication of the guilt I am trying to avoid. So, because I hate the guilt that is in me and have denied and projected that hate, I must also hate the person who reminds me that it's there. In the chicken's love this is called a love-hate relationship.

Also, we need to be aware that sacrifice is one of the basic pillars of the chicken's love. In the chicken's philosophy, when you give you lose. Remember, we begin from the position of lack, of feeling that there is something missing inside of us, so that we need something outside to make us complete. Thus, whenever we give, we feel a sense of loss, but we give anyway, because we have the illusory hope that, if we can just give and sacrifice enough, we will get back what we gave plus much more.

However, this kind of giving creates a sense of obligation in the other person. For example, giving can be a subtle means of manipulation. If I give and give and give to you without allowing you to give back to me, I've got you. I now have every right to make the statement: "I don't know why you do this to

---

[17] **From a Chicken to an Eagle,** pp. 17-20.

me! Look at all I've done for you." Now, don't misunderstand. Giving is not a bad thing to do. In fact, the act of giving itself is neutral. It takes on positive or negative results based on where we are coming from when we give something. In other words, whether we are based in the chicken's philosophy or the eagle's philosophy will determine whether our gift is an expression of real love or an effort to fill an inner lack.

Further, because the chicken's way of love is motivated by lack, making us feel that giving is losing, then the volume or quantity of our gifts becomes very important in showing us whether or not we are loved. And we are using the word "gifts" to refer not only to material things but also to less tangible things, such as time spent together, number of telephone calls, and so forth. How much we give other people in our lives becomes a way of reassuring them that all is well. The more we meet each other's needs, the deeper our love will feel. And, if we give enough and the delicate balance we create is maintained, then we have found for ourselves "a marriage made in heaven" — that is, according to the chicken.

In conclusion, let me offer a word of caution. Because the world we live in is based on the chicken philosophy of life, the chicken's idea of love has become the accepted idea of what love really is. So all relationships begin with the chicken's way of seeing love: all relationships begin as special relationships, in which we need someone or something outside of us to make us feel worthwhile.

Just because we live in this world and have accepted the chicken's philosophy of love, there is no need to feel guilty about it once we begin to understand what has been happening. It is necessary for everyone to grow up in this world and to learn the chicken's way of life and love. It is only after we have operated our lives on this premise and experienced the results over a period of time that we can make another choice for ourselves. Carl Jung once said, "Every problem after the age of thirty-five is a spiritual problem." The implication is that the prerequisite to spiritual unfoldment is "being in the world." The world is our classroom. We accept the programmed beliefs of our society (the chicken philosophy), live them out in our lives, see the results (pain and suffering), and then have the opportunity to make another choice, the eagle.

Ken Wapnick describes this process in this way:

> *The first half of our life is spent developing the tools of survival, learning to cope with the physical, psychological and social world, and can be thought of as a period of preparation. This period is natural in our human lives. Not to develop a personal identity or sense of self (ego) [chicken] leads to psychosis and, in extreme cases, autism. It is a paradox of our human lives that we must spend this first part of our lives in developing an ego, which we must then unlearn in the second part. The second stage involves implementing these abilities and skills, answering the question: which master do we follow? God or the ego [the chicken or the eagle]. There is a developmental readiness for*

> *spiritual learning. True spiritual maturity is not possible until we come of age.*[18]

Remember that fifty-year-old woman who thought of herself as a failure? When I responded to her, it was one of those times when what I said wasn't coming from me. "You're *not* a failure, you are really a success," I said to her, and that was exactly right. Until we get to the point which she had reached, where we are successful at doing something (the chicken's way) which just plain doesn't work, and experience the results (pain and suffering), we will never see that we can make another choice (the eagle).

So it is important not to think we have been wrong nor to feel guilty because we live in the world and need other people. This book is *not* against special relationships; rather its purpose is to explain how special relationships are developed based on fear, to show the results of continuing to hold on to them, and then to suggest another way (the eagle's way) of looking at special relationships that can move us toward freedom and joy and peace, toward discovering who we really are.

[18] **Forgiveness and Jesus**, pp. 111-112.

CHAPTER 10

THE EAGLE'S WAY OF LOVE

Let us briefly review the three basic principles which underlie the chicken's way of love; then, as we turn to look more deeply at the eagle's way of love, we will even more easily be able to see the vast difference between the two. Remember, the chicken wants us to operate from the basis of lack: his first and basic principle for us is that we lack something and are incomplete. From this point, it is a short step to the second principle, that we need something to compensate for that lack, and we are quickly convinced that only by looking outside of ourselves can we find a person or thing that will fill that lack and incompleteness. Once we have found this person or thing, a special relationship develops, the person or thing now becomes our source of self-worth and "OK-ness," and we soon become dependent upon the relationship. Ultimately, the dependency results in resentment and hostility, which leads us back to guilt, the basis of the chicken's philosophy.

But if we follow the eagle's way, this whole process never gets off the ground. In the first place, the eagle wants to us to know that we lack nothing, we have everything, and we are everything. Secondly, because we lack nothing, we have no need of anything, and therefore, there is no necessity to search outside of ourselves for a special relationship. Consequently, we do not build a dependency on something outside of ourselves, so we feel no hostility, and we never complete the circle back to feeling guilt.

Let me explain this in another way. If you and I accept the philosophy of the eagle, then I cannot give you love the way I would give you a pencil or a book that you needed. If I try to give you love, this presupposes both that you lack love and that I have the power to give it to you. But remember, you are complete and whole: you do not lack anything, including love. I can't give you something you already have and are, which is love.Thus, in the eagle's philosophy, I can't give you love the way I could give you a pencil, but I can *be loving*.

Being loving involves a totally different process from the one at work in the chicken's philosophy. For me to be loving, I must first accept the fact that I am love and have love within me. Once I am willing to begin to move the blocks out of the way of love's presence within me, that love naturally begins to move toward you. When I come from this understanding, I recognize that you, too, are a being of love and that your feelings that you lack love are really a call for help. Thus, I am able to relate to you in such a way that I support your capacity to discover the power of love and strength in you.

In the eagle's way of love, love is not something you can learn about; rather, it is the Truth about you as a person. You *are* Love. Love is how you are created, and it is your natural inheritance. All you need to do is move the obstacles of guilt, fear, anger out of the way to its presence. Let's now look at how this is done in the eagle's way of love.

When I follow the chicken's way of falling in love, what I fall in love with is your capacity to meet my needs. In contrast, the eagle's way of love says that when I fall in love, I fall in love with the other person's capacity to be a mirror for me, to show me what I have been unable to see about myself, that I am a child of love. He or she becomes the person from whom I will learn forgiveness and to whom I will teach forgiveness. Thus, the other person becomes my learning partner and, at the same time, my teacher. When I follow the eagle's way of love, every thing, person and event in my life is my teacher.

To illustrate how a special relationship becomes a mirror which allows us to see what needs healing within us, let us return to our earlier illustration of how special relationships worked with the chicken: let's assume once again that I am hoping to find a special relationship. As we have pointed out, the world we live in is based on the chicken's philosophy, and we quite normally find ourselves seeking for love and happiness by turning to someone or something out there in the world. Thus, my search will begin in exactly the same way: one day, I notice you, become interested, and decide to ask you for a date so that I can get to know you. And quite possibly, you are seeking the same thing, and so you agree to a date.

Our early encounters seem to develop in just the same way as before, with each of us deriving more and more pleasure from the other's company, spending a great deal of energy on pleasing the other, enjoying the intensity and wonder of getting to know another human being. But, because I am still new to the ways of the eagle, I am beginning to feel happier and more complete than I did before; in fact, I am probably even putting a few of my security eggs into your basket. This all feels wonderful, of course, and if it could go on like this forever, we might very well wonder what could possibly be wrong. In such a case, the wise would say: "If it ain't broke, don't fix it."

But the problem is that it never does go on forever. Sooner or later, one of us feels a first little twinge of dissatisfaction or displeasure with one of our partner's actions. Let's assume it's that simple matter of the missed phone call: you had been calling me, quite happily and voluntarily, eight times a day, but one day you only called five times. My reaction, just as before, is a combination of irritation — after all, I waited for the calls when I could have done something else — and guilt — what did I do to make you forget to call?

Here is the point where the appearance of similarities between the two situations ends and where we can begin to understand the great contrasts between the basic philosophies. For I can now recognize those feelings of irritation and guilt as the warning signals they truly are. If I re-examine the situation, projecting the film through the eagle's projector, and practice forgiveness, it suddenly appears in a very different light. Now I can take back the responsibility for my happiness that I had begun to hand to you, and I can realize that I am complete and whole, whether you call or not. You do not subtract from who I am if you don't call as often as I would like. Moreover, I can see you, not as someone who is trying to irritate or anger me, but rather as a being of love, just as I am, who is similarly trying to live the best life possible.

Through practicing forgiveness, I have brought that irritation and guilt back into my own mind, where it originated. Then I have decided not to see your actions as a threat to me. After all, I made the choice to wait at home for your call, and I know that I have done nothing in this relationship that was not loving. So if I have not been attacked by you, then I have no need to feel irritation or guilt at your behavior. Now my response to you can be a truly loving response. And I can be grateful to you for giving me the opportunity to see something about myself that I want to change.

Remember, back in the chicken's way of love, the process of growing and deepening in love meant that we both were getting better and better at meeting each other's needs. The more those needs were met, the deeper we felt our love was. Conversely, whenever we felt any lessening of attention from our partner, we felt that love being threatened and we struggled to find a way to make things be as they had been. But, as we saw, what we really did was to bury the love we always had, the love we always were, under layers and layers of guilt and fear.

Now, by following the eagle's way, we wake up to our true natures. We find that the people and situations in our lives become the opportunity to remove these layers. This is like peeling an onion. The more we practice forgiveness, the more layers of the onion are peeled off. As we continue to learn our lessons and more layers peel off, the light of love, which has been there all along, shines through more and more brightly. And the brighter that light becomes, the more we can experience that love.

As we learn the eagle's lessons, we see more and more clearly that we are all united and bonded together in love. Our love seems to grow and deepen because we are getting better and better at learning how to forgive — ourselves and others. The light in us has fewer and fewer barriers of guilt to shine through. However, we must remember that, when we follow the eagle's way, our love is not really growing, because love doesn't grow, it just is. What is happening instead is that we are "ungrowing" in guilt.

Finally, there are two additional characteristics that will help to distinguish special love based on the chicken's philosophy from Real Love according to the Eagle. The first of these is that special love is always an exclusive phenomenon. In its focus on one special person or thing, it always excludes other people; thus, it seems to find some people better and more valuable than other people. In contrast, the Real Love of the Eagle is all-inclusive. Because we are love, when we are being true to our nature, we feel love for all others. The Eagle makes no exceptions. As the Bible says, God has no favorites.

The second characteristic is a corollary of the first. As we look at our world, especially through the eyes of the chicken, it would seem that some people are better than others, more deserving of our love.

But the Eagle shows us that we are *all* special and equal. We are all the same, all learners, although we may look different in our own experiences of learning.

So we can conclude that the Eagle's way of love operates from the following principles: (1) Most important, we lack nothing, have and are everything. (2) As we choose the eagle's way of love, we begin falling in love with another's capacity to be our teacher; that other person becomes the person from whom we learn forgiveness and to whom we teach it. Thus, every person and situation becomes an opportunity for us to practice forgiveness. (3) In the chicken's way of love, special relationships are always exclusive; but the eagle's way of love always includes everybody. (4) We are all united and bonded together in love; practicing forgiveness peels back the layers of guilt to the point where the love which is what we really are can begin to shine through in our own experience.

PART IV

SPIRITUALITY: AN ILLUSION OR THE REAL TRUTH

CHAPTER 11

THE CHICKEN'S WAY OF SPIRITUALITY OR THE ILLUSION OF BEING SPIRITUAL

To open this chapter, I would like to ask for your active participation in a simple two-part exercise. First, after some consideration, how do you answer this question: Are you a spiritual person? It doesn't matter whether your answer is yes or no; the point is to consider the topic of spirituality. For the second part of this little exercise, put this book aside for a few minutes, find a piece of paper and a pen or pencil, and make a list of the criteria that you feel would make a person spiritual.

Now, I assume that you've made your list and you're back. Of course, this is an exercise for which there are no right or wrong answers, but let me share with you some responses made by persons who were asked the same question by me at workshops I have conducted. The items on their lists included:

- be loving
- go to church
- read the Bible
- pray
- sacrifice
- meditate
- don't be angry
- be pleasing to God
- achieve inner peace
- do good deeds so you can get into heaven
- be careful not to sin because you will be punished

The one thread that runs through these items — and through most of the items on all of the lists — was a confusion as to how the person conceived of God and their spiritual behavior. On the one hand, He seemed to be a God of Love, the Father of the prodigal son, but on the other hand He was a God of Anger, the punishing Father of the Garden of Eden. Many of the lists would lean toward one or the other, but in most, there were characteristics of both concepts of God within the implied definitions of spirituality.

These two ideas about God are, of course, diametrically opposed to each other, and yet we often try to hold both concepts in our minds when we think about God and about how we should behave in order to be spiritual. It is very difficult to hear about a God Who will cast us into eternal hell for our sins, and then to read the story of the Loving Father, Who waits patiently for His prodigal son to come home and, when he does, has no words of condemnation for him but only open arms of love.

What we have done, clearly, is to mix together these two unmixable concepts. It is like trying to mix oil and water: each liquid is clear and transparent when poured into a jar, but they remain distinct and separate. To mix them, we must thoroughly shake the container, breaking each liquid up into tiny bubbles that seem to be mixed together. But the resulting mixture is very cloudy, not at all transparent, and if we wait a few moments, we see that the two liquids have not mixed at all but have settled back out as separate liquids. Our concepts of God are similar: an Angry God is understandable — not pleasant, of course, but recognizable — and we know how to behave to please Him. After all, that is how we human beings tend to behave: cross us and we'll getcha. And the idea of a Loving God is also clear to us, although we seem less likely, as human beings, to display the behavior of a Loving God in our daily lives. Nevertheless, each concept, separately, is understandable and clear. What happens, however, is that we shake these two concepts up and try to mix them together in our heads, and all that results is confusion and cloudiness. And that just doesn't work. God can't be an angry god and a loving God at the same time. We cannot have a little bit of hell in heaven or a little bit of heaven in hell. One concept must be true and the other must be false.

The way to clear up this confusion, then, is to examine each way of looking at spirituality, so that we can see just how diametrically opposed they are to each other. We will begin by looking at the concept that God is an angry God. This is the idea that is held by the chicken, and it underlies his whole system of spirituality. Remember, the chicken's system is based on the story of Adam and Eve and has as its foundation an angry God who is intent on punishing us. All the ideas of spirituality that the chicken presents to us and that we will examine in this chapter are based on this premise.

Remember, the reason we believe God wants to punish us is that we think we are inherently and basically sinners, because we have done something wrong which we feel is unforgiveable. But, since this concept of ourselves is not very pleasant to live with, we are motivated to create another self that hides and detracts from that horrible self. Clearly, this self should appear to be whole and good, the very opposite of how we think of our real self. In fact, to be specific, we would like this made-up self to appear to be very spiritual. Naturally, since we feel we are really evil, we must look outside of ourselves to find the material with which to create this façade.

The chicken, who never once misses an opportunity to put more barriers between us and the Truth, is quick to suggest that one way we can build this spiritual self is by working very hard to be what others consider a "good person." Further, he suggests that there are several ways of going about doing this. One is to be sure that we don't make others angry at us. People get angry at those who are bad and/or do bad things, not at spiritual people. Therefore, if we are successful at not making people angry, we have an unconscious hope that this will prove we aren't bad, that we will be classified as "good people." And, if we're really good — i.e., really spiritual — perhaps that angry God will get this message.

Another suggestion the chicken makes to help us create a spiritual self is to tell us that there is a "right" pathway to follow, certain things we can do that will make us appear to be moving in the right direction, to have it all together. So we read the Bible, we go to this church, we pray, we follow that guru, we meditate, we fast, we go to a different church, we become vegetarians, we chant, we switch to a "righter" guru, we do yoga, etc. We go through all the forms, always hoping that we can appear to be "good enough" by doing enough of the right spiritual actions to offset our inner sense of being a horrible sinner. At the deepest level, we are still terrified and convinced that we will not succeed either in escaping God's wrath or in convincing Him that we don't really deserve to be punished. Nevertheless, we work hard at creating an illusion of being spiritual through the use of these "right" forms and rituals.

Malcolm Boyd, in **The Book of Days**, describes the result of this effort to do everything the "right" way and acquire all the "right" things. He, like most of us, received constant messages from the world outside of him about how he should live, the different things he should have.

> *I decided to try them. Not everything, but the right ones. Ad men would henceforth be my prophets. They talked about such pleasant things, always on the bright side — except for the day when the postman would leave the bills. But, the ad men said, pay by installments. I bought the right car, the right gin, the right suits, the right TV sets, the right chocolates, the right deodorants, the right coffee, the right suppositories and the right life insurance. I switched to the right cigarette, the right newspaper, the right vermouth, the right church, the right suntan ointment, the right undergarment, the right news magazine and the right airline. And what did I find? Milk and honey? My image and I are now exact. I'm no longer me. . . . I'm "it."* [19]

Finally, the chicken confides to us the third and most important step we can take to cover up our

[19] Malcolm Boyd, **The Book of Days**, Random House, 1968.

vileness. If we truly want to look spiritual, we must find a way to sacrifice something of ourselves for others. This is the ultimate behavior, insists the chicken, by which we will appease God's anger, fill the void within us, and be able, at last, to stop hiding and living in guilt and fear.

Now, if we have accepted the basic premise of the chicken philosophy, that we are sinners and lack something inside of us, the idea of sacrifice makes perfect sense. It's simple, the chicken says: if you are willing to sacrifice something of yourself for someone else, this will be proof that you love that other person. The other person will then see what a wonderful, giving person you are and will give back love to you, which will fill your lack. We see this idea portrayed all around us, in movies, on television, in popular songs, in novels. The message is clear: if we sacrifice, that is, if we give up part of ourselves, our time, our money, or whatever, for someone or something else, we are showing real love and dedication. Parents who "go without" so that their children won't have to, the lover who is constantly giving up time for the beloved, the worker who puts aside personal desires to meet company demands: all of these actions, we insist, are done in the name of love.

But then the results start coming in: the children don't appreciate what they've been given, leaving the parents deprived and bitter. The lover sees the beloved go off with another, in spite of every effort to please, and there is more bitterness. The worker, expecting at the very least retirement benefits, is left out in the cold and out of a job because the company has merged with another. We can all tell our stories, in which we have given out of love and later have been disappointed. But it is that very disappointment that signals that we are operating from the chicken's perspective.

The chicken's formula is that, if we give up something of ourselves in a spirit of sacrifice, we will appear to be spiritual, good, complete — in a word, lovable — and then we will get back what we have given, with increase. What we don't understand is that giving in this way — sacrificing, as the chicken's spirituality demands — is based on giving to get, that behind whatever we give lies our hidden hope that we will receive what we lack and thus erase, or at least cover over, our sin. But when we give to get, instead of filling a lack within us, we increase it; giving of ourselves in this manner takes away from ourselves, and there is never a guarantee that we will receive what we expect.

On the following pages, in Diagrams 4A and 4B, you will find a chart which lays out these ideas we have been discussing in a step-by-step format. Each of the chicken's suggested actions is listed on the left, in Diagram 4A, with the behavior he is recommending to us, and his explanation of why we should do as he says. But on the right hand page, in Diagram 4B, for each of these steps we find the Truth, the reason why the chicken's logic just does not work. Of course, the ideas on this side of the chart will be examined in much greater detail when we go on to the next chapter on the eagle's way of spirituality. But for now, the

THE CHICKEN'S WAY OF SPIRITUALITY
THE ILLUSION OF BEING SPIRITUAL

THE STEPS TO SPIRITUALITY	WHAT WE NEED TO DO	THE CHICKEN'S LOGIC
1 NOTICE THERE IS A LACK	Recognize that something is missing inside of us, and we feel unloved. So we need to fill this lack.	We made God angry, so He is no longer in our lives. It is this absence of God that makes us feel we have a lack.
2 FILL THE LACK	We must start looking for some way to provide ourselves with the love that we feel is missing.	God is no longer in our lives because of our sin. We have to find some way to fill that space, to feel loved again.
3 LOOK OUTSIDE	If we lack something inside, we obviously won't find it there. We must turn to something or someone outside of ourselves.	If we look inside, we will see our guilt — and that is terrifying. So we must turn outside to find our happiness: if someone or something outside can make us feel loved, we won't miss God's love.
4 SACRIFICE	We can't expect someone from the outside to just fill our needs, so we will have to sacrifice something of ourselves. We hope we will get back not only what we have given, but even more — and thus we will fill the lack.	Sacrifice is equal to love: we know how much others love us by how much they are willing to sacrifice for us. Also, if we are willing to sacrifice and suffer, this will help absolve some of our guilt. Surely then God will see that we are really good, and we will win back His love.
5 BE A SPIRITUAL PERSON	We must earnestly follow all of the steps above, especially the last one. Sacrifice and suffering are the measure of our goodness. We must work hard to do the right things, to appear complete. We must be long suffering and as saintly as possible.	We have made God angry, so our real self must be bad. We must create a new self that can replace the tainted self. We must become spiritual, sacrificing so that God will someday love us again and take us back. The more we give up for others, the more loving we will seem.

Diagram 4A

THE TRUTH

THE CHICKEN'S STEPS TO SPIRITUALITY	THE REAL TRUTH ABOUT THE CHICKEN'S SPIRITUALITY
1 NOTICE THERE IS A LACK	God is not angry — and never has been. He is always present in our lives with His love, so there is not lack.
2 FILL THE LACK	Trying to fill this lack the chicken is pointing to is like trying to fill a cup that is already full to the brim. There is no lack, so we have no need to spend time and effort trying to fill it. We are created as love, so we already have everything and are everything.
3 LOOK OUTSIDE	To keep us looking outside of ourselves is the way the chicken makes sure that we accept his perception of who we are: sinners. Once we are willing to see that we have chosen to do this, we can choose through the process of forgiveness, to see the real Truth about ourselves; we are Love, Peace, Joy and Light.
4 SACRIFICE	Sacrifice is giving to get. We give up parts of ourselves for others hoping to be loved and thus fill that lack we've decided is there inside us. Hidden behind our sacrifice, however, is hate, because we will inevitably not receive what we hope to get, and we will then become angry. Nevertheless, we sacrifice, because we hope to put ourselves back into God's good graces. But the Truth is we have done nothing to God. He is waiting inside of us to welcome us Home — we need merely to wake up from our bad dream and realize this Truth.
5 BE A SPIRITUAL PERSON	Our real selves, the children of Love who we truly are, have been covered over with a veil of guilt, We have shown the world our false selves, created to try to prove to all — including God — that we are not bad, that we deserve to be forgiven and allowed to come back Home. But all of our efforts are unnecessary. We are already truly spiritual beings, needing only to discover and accept this Truth. The Loving Father simply waits for us to give Him our fear, anger, and guilt, so that He can shine them away. Being a spiritual person is merely accepting the Truth of Love about ourselves.

Diagram 4B

chart can summarize for us the way the chicken's system of spirituality works.

After examining this chart, it may occur to us to wonder why, when the concept of "sacrifice" has so many unpleasant aspects to it, we continue to do it so constantly. The answer becomes clear when we examine our deepest motives once again. Remember that the idea which gives sacrifice its power in our lives is the haunting fear we have that God is going to punish us. This fear is so powerful that we are willing to make a bargain with Him. If we sacrifice for another, thereby giving up some of our own satisfaction and bringing suffering into our lives now, then maybe He won't be so hard on us later. To put it another way, we hope that if we suffer enough, this may get us back in His good graces.

We can see ourselves clearly in the story of the prodigal son. After the son has decided to return home, he begins thinking about what he will say to his father. Because he expects his father to be angry and to punish him, the son begins to wonder what he can do to get back in the father's good graces. He finally comes up with what he thinks will be the best plan. If his father will just allow him to come back home, he will give up being his son and just be a servant. He hopes that, by giving up his rightful place in his father's house, he will have made enough of a sacrifice that he will at least be allowed back into the household again.

Thus, when we follow the chicken's idea of spirituality, which he presents to us as our salvation, we are urged to put on an *appearance* of spirituality through our actions in the world outside of us. Although we feel at bottom that we are evil, guilty, and deserving of punishment, the chicken tells us that we can try to hide these miserable qualities behind a façade of goodness and spirituality. And he makes it clear that the quickest way to erect that façade is to sacrifice ourselves for others. It is only through sacrifice, he insists, that we will appear to those around us — including God, when He catches up with us — to be worthy of their love and thus will be able to fill the emptiness inside. In truth, what we are doing is creating merely the *illusion* of being spiritual.

CHAPTER 12

THE EAGLE'S WAY OF SPIRITUALITY

As was described in the last chapter, the chicken's way of spirituality is based on the premise that we are sinners and have a fatal flaw. We feel this is our real self. The chicken does not want us to look closely at this belief, because if we did, we might see past it and find out it's not true. If this were to happen, of course, the chicken's game would be over. Thus, the chicken instructs us to create a new self to show to the world — a "good" self — to draw attention away from this "bad" self. So all of our efforts in life are to make the world believe that we aren't "all that bad," and to hide from the world how bad we think we really are.

All of this changes in the eagle's way of spirituality. Now we begin with the basic premise that we are all children of Love. We have been created Love because this is what the essence of our Loving Father really is, and we are extensions of His creative Love. We have nothing of sin in us, and we are not flawed; in fact, we are whole, complete, and perfect. We cover up and forget this Truth about ourselves when we believe in the chicken's perception of who we are. That misplaced belief is the only barrier stopping us from discovering and accepting who we really are.

We are like the son, referred to earlier, who thinks he is having a nightmare. The horrors he dreams seem insurmountable, but he seeks desperately to find a way to overcome them. But it is clear to his Father, Who watches him in love, that he need only awaken to end the terror he is experiencing and which seems so real. Thus, the only barrier between him and peace is his own belief in that nightmare. The Course in Miracles uses two additional analogies to describe this situation. In one place, we read, "We are at Home in God, dreaming of exile," and at another place, "we are on a journey without distance, to a goal that has never changed." [20]

Obviously, then, in the eagle's way of spirituality, there is no need to create another "better" self to hide behind, in hopes that we can fool the world. All we need is the willingness both to see that the chicken's way of life only brings us pain and suffering and also to be willing to move these blocks of fear, anger and guilt out of the way so that we can allow the Love that we are to shine through.

This process, this "way Home," is what was described earlier as forgiveness. Forgiveness is the basic principle of the Eagle's way of spirituality, and, as with anything else, the more we practice forgiveness, the more easily we can move the blocks out of the way and begin to wake up to who we really are. It isn't easy at first. We must remember that we have been practicing the chicken's way of spirituality for years and years, until by now it has become an unconscious belief and habit. Our aim is to begin to change this belief and habit by substituting a new way of perceiving. In order to do this, we must be alert to our opportunities: anytime we experience the old

---

[20] The Course in Miracles, **Text**, pp. 169 and 139, respectively, Foundation for Inner Peace, Box 635, Tiburon, California.

familiar feelings of fear, anger, guilt, confusion, whatever, we have the chance to practice forgiveness. All we need is to be willing to see the old habit, say "No" to it, and then ask for help to see things through the eyes of Love — and we must practice this over and over. The more we practice it, the more natural forgiveness will become.

It's like the illustration used earlier about learning to play the piano. A prospective pianist begins by practicing scales, watching fingers on keys until the point is reached where it is not necessary to watch the keys at all. At this point, playing feels natural and flowing, though the pianist is not yet a professional, by any means. Similarly with practicing the eagle's way of spirituality, forgiveness: this is not a practicing that makes "perfect" but a practicing that keeps us open to hearing the Messenger sent into our nightmare to help us see the happy dream of love and peace.

Let's now look at some of the basic characteristics of the eagle's way of spirituality. Remember, the temple of the eagle is not the body but relationships. I have seen many people in my practice who tell me all the spiritual activities they are into, all of the rituals they go through on their paths to spirituality. All of these are fine, but I always ask them the same question: "How are you getting along with your brothers and sisters? How are the relationships with your wife, your children, your mother and father, your boss, or any of the other people you deal with every day?" It is in these relationships that the eagle's way reaches its full expression.

For healing takes place only in the context of relationships. Each of us is at a different place in our growth, and therefore our paths will all look very different. But if we are heading Home by following the eagle's way of spirituality, we will find a basic theme common to all paths: we are all Children of Love, and we demonstrate that by bringing healing to our relationships. Where we might have been guarded or resentful or angry or suspicious in dealing with our spouse or child or another, we now can act in a spirit of love and forgiveness.

Another characteristic of the eagle's way of spirituality is that there is no sacrifice. Because we are, in essence, Love and One with our Loving Father, we have everything and are everything and can lack nothing. We need not sacrifice or suffer to get back in good graces with our Father, because we have now discovered, like the prodigal son, that He only waits patiently for us to accept His open arms and to wake up from our terrifying nightmare. We need do nothing to earn His love; all that is necessary is that we accept that we have created that nightmare, and through forgiveness that we hear that inner Messenger of love that helps us bring our darkness of guilt into the light of His Love so that it will be shone away.

There is one final characteristic to note. When we open ourselves to who we really are, we won't hear trumpets blaring or angels singing, nor will the clouds open up. Rather, we will say, with surprise, "So it was you all the time." There is nothing exotic or mystical about the eagle's way, there are no special rites or rituals to perform, and we will not appear on the surface to be any different from our former selves.

But, as we follow the eagle's path of forgiveness, how will we know if it's working? The answer was supplied centuries ago by Jesus: "By their fruits ye shall know them." There will be at least four results, four "fruits," of our walking in the eagle's way. First, we will find ourselves becoming more peaceful inside, more patient, and less defensive. Second, we will find ourselves being less critical and condemning of others. Third, we will find those around us becoming more at peace with themselves. Our friends will have the pleasant experience of being more peaceful merely by being in our presence. Finally, we will all find ourselves smiling more — not at all the least significant of the fruits of our willingness to practice forgiveness.

CONCLUSION

We have been living in a bad dream, a nightmare of our own making. We have really believed there is truth in what the chicken philosophy teaches us:

1. *There is something basically wrong with us.*
2. *We have a fatal flaw.*
3. *We are in essence sinners who deserve punishment.*
4. *Our Father is very angry with us and demands sacrifice.*

We have lived our lives based on these assumptions, and we keep having the same results: fear, anger, guilt, suffering, pain, separation.

Maybe, like the prodigal son, we have become tired of being separated, living a nightmare in the far country. Maybe it's time to go home, to begin to wake up. But we are terrified, because we really believe what the chicken has told us, that we will be met by an angry Father Who waits to punish us.

We must remember that Loving Father, sitting by his sleeping son's bed, Who has sent a messenger into the nightmare, into the far country. The Father speaks to His son as he sleeps, saying, "What the chicken tells you about Me is not true. Listen, instead, to my messenger, who knows a way to find the truth. He calls it forgiveness."

Practicing forgiveness moves us from our nightmare of fear, anger, and guilt to the unfolding of a happy dream of love, peace, joy, and freedom. We will awaken in the arms of that Loving Father. Practicing forgiveness is the path that leads us from our feeling of separation in a far country to the waiting Presence of our Loving Father.

MR. JERRY FANKHAUSER, M.S.W., is in private practice as a psychotherapist in Houston, Texas. Along with doing individual, marital, and family therapy, he also conducts workshops in the area of personal growth and development. He is a member of the American Association of Marriage and Family Therapists, the National Association of Social Workers, and the American Society of Group Psychotherapy and Psychodrama.

Mr. Fankhauser has written three other books, **EVERYBODY IS YOUR TEACHER, FROM A CHICKEN TO AN EAGLE**, and **THE POWER OF AFFIRMATIONS**. In his writings and his practice, Mr. Fankhauser brings together the spiritual and psychological aspects of the person and sees the result of this merger to be spiritual psychotherapy.

If you wish to contact the author personally, he may be reached at the following address:

Mr. Jerry Fankhauser, M.S.W.
2650 Fountainview, Suite 208
Houston, Texas 77057

713-783-7264

To receive discount coupons toward your next purchase of these and other books and tapes, along with information about our newsletter, please send your name and address to the publisher listed below.

Miracle Publishing Company, Inc.
18 Charleston North
Sugarland, Texas 77478

713-242-4352